Single Mama Dos and Don'ts

To McCookie

A Super
grandmother ?

Amber,
A Super
Single
Mama

Single Mama Dos and Don'ts

KELLY WILLIAMS

Foreword by T. Winston Shaw
(Author's Son)

A singlemamahood Publishing Book

A singlemamahood Publishing Book

Editorial, sales and distribution, rights and permissions inquiries should be addressed to singlemamahood Publishing, 6335 N. Wayne Avenue, Chicago, IL 60660 www.singlemamahood.com

Manufactured in the United States of America
10 9 8 7 6 5 4 3 2 1

ISBN-13: 978-0-9789541-0-9
ISBN-10: 0-9789541-0-6

Library of Congress Control Number: 2006907983

First Edition

Contents

Foreword

I think that too many people make the mistake of approaching parenting as if to follow a clear-cut, scientific formula will ensure the gradual production of the perfect offspring. My mother has always known that childrearing is too complex to be viewed with a "one-size fits all" mentality. She understands that raising a child is like creating a piece of art; it takes patience and perspective. There will be times along the way when you may think that the piece of art into which you have been pouring your heart and soul isn't developing into what you had envisioned it to be. There will be times when you will wonder if all of the work that you have put in will ever pay off. You will wonder if others will ever see the beauty and depth that you see when you look at the canvas.

A parent must understand that well-raised children, like wondrous works of art, come in a diverse variety of forms. What one person sees as flawed or unappealing, another person may see as perfect or beautiful. After a certain amount of time, a child, like a great piece of art, takes on a presence and significance all his or her own. Parents can only hope that they have used all of the right elements of art in the development of their offspring.

My mother has always been a beacon of inspiration in my life. She has been unwaveringly supportive of me at every stage of my development. As I continue to grow and mature, I only come to appreciate more and more what she has so often selflessly given of herself time and time again in order to ensure my success. She has always managed to make me feel special without making me feel more important than anyone else. She has established within me a deep concern for others, and taught me by example to be loving, gracious, God-fearing, and forgiving. She has taught me that life is not supposed to be easy, and that though nothing in this world is promised, everything under the stars is within my reach.

Though I am my mother's only child, "Ms Kelly" has been a mother to so many sons and daughters. To anyone within her reach in need, Kelly Williams has been an open book and a pair of open arms, offering confidence, compassion, love, and discipline. She has been a second mother to more young people than I can remember, even opening up her own home to clothe and feed someone in need. She is the most incredible and amazing woman I know for more reasons than I can count.

Along the journey of raising a child, my mother has had the insight and vision to constantly enhance my maturation process. This hasn't always been easy, and she has often had to make tough decisions that she knew would in the end benefit my development.

One of the most important strategic parenting choices she made was to always foster a positive relationship between my father and me. She always separated her relationship with my father from my relationship with him. No matter what issues existed between my parents, she always maintained her dignity when discussing my father with me. She innately understood that a developing black child desperately needs a positive male role model. Though my mother never led me to believe the illusion that he (or she for that matter) was perfect, she softly encouraged me to see good in him.

As I am now a man, I realize that it is not perfection or flawlessness that makes a great parent, but the ability to master and overcome flaws and imperfections.

Kelly Williams pours her heart out in the form of advice time after time; she has been so much to so many for so long. She yearns to touch children's lives with wisdom for single mothers.

I just yearn to make my mother proud.

T. Winston Shaw
(Author's Son)

Acknowledgments

My heartfelt thanks to my wonderful, supportive, loving family and friends.

Winston, you are my inspiration. Stay focused and gain strength from your struggles.

To my Lord and Savior, Jesus Christ, for giving me a sign and the courage to step out on faith to use my gifts and talents to do your work.

For Jewel Kelley and Dr Leon Kelley

Introduction

"There's a little boy I know, his name is Winston. His mommy calls him Spoochie; his daddy calls him, Son. His babysitter, Oppie, calls him Bam-Bam, and when Granddaddy sees him, he says, Hey Winston, how' you doin' Boy? Give me five. Alright!"

I smile and get teary eyed when I think back to that little song I made up for my son, Winston, when he was a baby. He's 20 now, a sophomore in college. And he is quite a young man, a politician, teacher or a preacher -- and a lawyer, too, in the making. He never says specifically what profession he's after. But I tell him I see him doing any number of great things. I'm just happy he wants to share his gifts and talents with others. I love that he is independent and wise, witty and creative – and that he understands that life offers opportunity and hope and that struggles serve to make you stronger.

When my first book, *Single Mamahood,* was published, Winston was about 10 or 11. Over the years, I would regularly teasingly remind him to behave for Mama's sake, that there's no way I could have an advice book for single moms out there and be credible as a speaker if he didn't act like he had some sense. Fortunately, Winston survived childhood and is a fine young man.

I wrote the first book after Rhonda Sonnenberg, a writer, author and friend, told me that she thought I had a powerful position and voice and that from what she saw, I had enough good material with all the advice she'd heard me share with other moms.

I have never claimed to be the expert on single parenting, but I have always been a pretty good observer, and I can't hold back when I see a parent saying or doing something that is either exceptionally wonderful or so awful that I know it might be harmful to his or her child. God gave me an incredible gift – the ability and audacity to say things that other people only think. And I, for whatever reasons, am able to speak up in such a manner that people know I mean well. And I do not hesitate to use this gift.

Most people who are trained in some aspect of parenting deal with families that are experiencing a crisis or are high-risk. To my knowledge, one cannot get a college degree in Positive Single Parenting. Good parenting comes from doing it, living it, watching it, breathing it, sharing it and learning first-hand. It comes from constantly talking and listening to other parents, your own parents, friends, psychologists, pediatricians and kids. It comes from the ability to be empathetic and remember what you felt, expected and believed when you were a child. It's the result of focusing on what you and others do right and wrong and constantly working to be better.

When I wrote my first book, I was a TV news reporter, as well as a single mama. I had a lot of exposure to parents of all kinds. My mother always told me that it's better to learn from the mistakes of others than to have to make them all yourself. So I thought the book thing was a pretty good idea. I would take what I'd learned from my own mistakes and those of others, and write about it in a manner that I hoped would serve others. Since then, I've learned a lot more, first-hand and otherwise. I've experienced parenting an adolescent, a teenager and now a young adult. If you're a mama in either of those phases, you know it is a constant learning process.

Single Mama Dos and Don'ts is a testament to the biggest lesson I've learned in the 8 years since writing that first book. That lesson is that despite what things might look like from the outside, moms from every walk of life, whether married or single, really do want to be good mothers. Some of us simply don't have the tools or even know where to begin. This book is designed to be a simple, user friendly, single mama's toolkit. So Mama, open your mind and drop your shoulders. You may not like everything you read, but trust me, this book is designed to make your life less drama-filled so that you can focus on your most important responsibility -- being the best mama you can be.

Single Mama Dos and Don'ts

1

Do Enjoy Every Phase Of Your Children's Lives. The Time Really Does Go By Quickly.

It was early, hours before the sun came up. My big belly made it hard for me to sleep. I was used to that. But something was different about this morning. I felt like I was having menstrual cramps. But it couldn't be. I was nine months pregnant.

I'd read about what to expect. I went to the toilet and sure enough. The plug they talked about, as gross as it sounded (and must seem to you reading this), really did disengage, just as the books had said it would. This was the day. September 25th, 1986. Somebody was fixing to be born.

"Hey," I said to my baby's daddy. I think this is it. I think I'm in labor."

"Are you sure?" he asked groggily. "Yeah," I replied.

Like many single mamas, I was shacking up with my soon-to-be-born child's father. Everything was so unplanned and disorganized. I, like so many of us, hoped I'd be married by then. But as is the case so often, there were a gazillion excuses and explanations for why I was still single. I would be joining the statistics of the unmarried mother population.

Mamas, if you are living with your baby's father, you, too, are a single mama. Do not get it twisted.

Back to my story. We'd had an appointment that morning with Dr. Sirmans, my Ob-GYN. When we went to see him, he confirmed what I thought. I was going to have my baby before that day ended. But I wasn't quite ready. Dr. Sirmans said I should go for a walk, maybe go see a movie, just let the time pass. He said I should not call him to meet me at the hospital until I could no longer speak. If you're a mama, you know that didn't register with me until that time actually came. If you're not a mama, but expecting, get ready, Miss Lady!

We went to see *Stand By Me*, a movie about a group of boys – friends who went through all kinds of adventures, getting into trouble, learning lessons, having fun and just being boys. It's kind of ironic now that in hindsight, after knowing of my son's childhood -- his adventures and misadventures -- and his buddies, friends in every city I dragged him to and from. Thanks to the Internet, they've all remained close, Louis (LJ), Chezeray (Ray-Ray), Jordan and later, Ayo -- the kids with whom he hung and sneaked around and formed lifelong memories. What a 20 years! The time went back so quickly. Throughout my child's youth, I think I heard people say more than a dozen times, "Enjoy your time with him now." "Enjoy this stage; it goes by so quickly." That is so true. I think the first "Single Mama Do" should be just that. So let me say it, myself, and explain to you exactly what I mean.

Enjoy Every Phase of your children's lives.
It really does go by quickly.

If you are a new mom, this will be the only *Do* that you'll really be able to sink your teeth into until later on.

Tanya

Tanya had been home from the hospital two weeks when she first began to feel it. It was something she tried so hard to ignore – something that made her feel a kind of guilt she'd never experienced before. It happened every time she'd fall into what seemed to be a deep sleep, except she could hardly remember what sleep was these days. It seems every time she finally fell into any kind of nap, her little Brandon was screaming at the top of his lungs. And Tanya's boyfriend, her baby's daddy, Ralph, would just sleep right through it.

In fact these were the times when Tanya pretty much knew that Ralph had to go. Forget the fact that he was selfish and would remind her on a regular basis that she lucky. She didn't have to work and was living free of change in "his house." Never mind that during her pregnancy and even now, he stayed out all hours of the night. Forget that he had more than nine months to get a divorce from his estranged other baby's mama, Desirae, and was always behind on his child support to her. As a matter of fact, when was the last time Ralph saw Jordan and Justine anyway? No wonder Desirae was always creating all the drama! Her twins had to eat. And it'd be nice if they could see their daddy every now and then.

At these times, Tanya felt what she'd never before experienced, a frustration, a guilt like no other – a longing to have her old self back. She was a slave to Brandon, this helpless little 7-pound 8-ounce needy, crying, helpless baby.

It was the weirdest feeling, too. The guilt was the result of the simple fact that she knew better. She had heard about postpartum depression and whatever else Brooke Shields experienced. But Brooke Shields is a rich celebrity who could afford nannies and housekeepers and spa weekends away from her husband, if that was what she needed. Tanya felt she had few choices.

Tanya was living in Atlanta when she and Ralph met. About a year later, he got a job in Charlotte, North Carolina, so they started seeing each other long distance. Tanya had a great job at MARTA and although she put in resumes for jobs in Charlotte, nothing had come through. That's when she found herself pregnant. How in the world could she have been so careless? And with her strict Christian upbringing, abortion was out of the question.

Tanya had her doubts when Ralph said she should just move to Charlotte. She'd be giving up her salary and benefits. But Ralph said that wouldn't be a problem; he'd marry her and put her on his insurance. She was glad she had enough savings to cover the high premium required through her COBRA plan. Even if Ralph had followed through, finalized his divorce with Desirae and married Tanya, his medical insurance would not have covered her pre-existing condition. She didn't think of that when Ralph was talking all that marriage game. But of course, it didn't matter now anyway. Half the stuff Ralph promised her didn't amount to much about now.

She felt claustrophobic, stuck in a place where she did not feel welcome, with no job, no friends and a newborn crying his eyes out. A newborn who was so cute, with his big dark brown eyes, long curly eyelashes, smooth, soft, baby-powder smelling skin, pretty little mouth – especially when it was not delivering those painful sounds that kept her up in the night. It's just that when she thought of where she was in her relationship with Ralph – which was really nowhere at all, the things about Brandon that made her feel tired and irritable and resentful, and yes, sometimes regretful – those were the things that occupied most of her thoughts about her baby. Oh, what a huge responsibility she had on her hands! What was she going to do?

Tanya remembered the last time she felt torn over decisions she had made. She had been offered a great job – the one at MARTA, in fact, when she graduated from Spelman. At the same time, she had been accepted to law school at Georgetown. No one in her family had ever been a lawyer. She would have been the first. But the money was so good at MARTA. She could finally buy a nice car and have a cool apartment and actually do more than window shop when she went to the mall. She took the job. But always, in the back of her mind, she wondered what things would have been like had she stuck it out and gone to law school. By now, she'd be done with school and would be making some serious bucks. Who knows, she may have felt strong enough to have ditched Mr. Ralph months ago. Or perhaps they never would have even met.

So here she was, changing diapers, trying like everything to get this stupid breast feeding down (From everything she had read about breast milk, she knew that this was best for her baby), rocking Brandon, singing to him, doing everything in her power to get him to go to sleep when he started all that screaming. How in the world could this possibly be something she should be enjoying?

Then one day, Tanya got an email from a woman she had worked with back in Atlanta. She was an older lady who got married when she was in her forties. The lady was telling Tanya that she, too, had a newborn; her baby was just five days old. She'd heard that Tanya had just given birth.

Before Tanya could read on, she was completely confused. She remembered this lady, Nancy, but could not recall her even being pregnant and no one she'd spoken with back at the job ever mentioned it. Then Tanya read on.

"Bruce and I never told anyone that we were waiting for a baby, that we had even planned to adopt. But I had undergone a hysterectomy when I was in my late 30s and I wanted more than anything in the world to have a child. Now, finally, I have my baby. Her name is Kimberly and you should see her. She's African American. We struggled with adopting a black child since we're both white. We wanted to make sure we were able to give an African American baby everything she'd need, emotionally and culturally. So we simply committed to doing just that. Attached is her photo, because there's no way I can do justice to describing how incredibly beautiful she is. She's lying here right now looking up at me. God, I wish I could breastfeed her. I actually read about women who are not birth mothers who work with their physicians and train their bodies so that they actually lactate. But that was, unfortunately, not an option for me.

Still I feel so great when she cries out for me in the night. I have not slept more than two hours straight since we picked her up from the hospital. I just feel so much like a mother!

Bruce is great; although I have to admit, he sleeps soundly when Kimberly cries. But I hear that's common with dads. I love being all that Kimberly really needs in the world right now. I cannot remember what my life was like before she came into it. It certainly wasn't this exciting. I'm

*going to enjoy ever moment with her, every week,
and every month. God has blessed me with her;
and I want to show Him my thanks and
appreciation in how I serve her and fulfill her
needs. I love motherhood!*

*Pardon this long email; I know we hardly know
one another. But I couldn't think of anyone else to
share my news with. Because you just gave birth,
I knew you'd be able to relate. So let's stay in
touch; tell me all about your baby. And send me a
photo. You had a boy, right?"*

Tanya sobbed when she finished the note. She
picked up Brandon and held him tight. From
that moment, she stopped kidding herself and
made plans to move on with her life – as a single
mama -- and to appreciate and enjoy it.

Tips for Enjoying the Moment

1. **Count your blessings; don't dwell on the
   negative.**
2. **Consider hardships a blessing, a lesson
   that makes you stronger and gives you
   courage and hope.**
3. **Know that there are many women who
   are praying right now for babies.**
4. **Understand that hard times are only a
   moment in time and as for any drama
   you're experiencing, it, too, shall pass.**

2

Do Surround Yourself With People Who Support You And Your Kids.

One thing single mamas know is that some people in their lives have NOT a clue. They don't get who you are, what you are about or what you have to deal with everyday. Some want to be around you for purely selfish reasons. My sister, Kerry, has a nickname for people like this. She calls them "users.com." Too many times, we surround ourselves with people who keep us from moving forward. A man in Mississippi with whom I've spoken about this who oversees a parental visitation enforcement program says this is all too common with single mamas – that misery still loves company.

For a number of reasons, we attract so-called friends who like to have pity parties with us, bring us down to their level instead of doing the hard work to lift themselves up so that they can be supportive of our attempts to work on ourselves. If you are a single mama, you cannot afford to spend your valuable time with people like this. So don't.

People you call friends should be those who care about your kids. In other words, you don't need to subject your children to people who rag on your children's daddies and/or constantly complain about their own messed up lives and "no good" babies' daddies. If people are so selfish or clueless that they disregard what they say in the presence of your kids, they don't care about you. If they are so simple that they do not know the harm they are doing, it's your job to help them understand and to tell them the negativity must cease. But first you must face this reality, yourself. (So when you finish reading this book, loan it to your friends, or better yet, buy them a copy of their own.)

Feeling guilty? Good. Nine times out of ten, it's because you know that the only reason you're surrounding yourself with negative people is that somehow, it feels comfortable. You let people say and do things around you that you know are not good for you or your family because you don't feel good enough about yourself to demand or expect anything different. Or maybe you're the one who really doesn't know any better. Maybe you don't feel you deserve any better, because ever since you were a little girl, people haven't had many good things to say about you.

Well guess what? You're a mother now, a grownup. Where there is life, there is hope. Sure, there are plenty of excuses for why it's hard to do this or seems impossible to do that. But know that whatever it is, success awaits you if you want it; you just have to believe it and work hard to get it. And it is possible with prayer and perseverance to do better. It may come in baby steps, and there might be some setbacks, but you can move forward. But it's a whole lot harder when you're towing dead weight behind you.

I just read an article in *Essence* about a young woman who grew up homeless but was determined to improve her life, no matter what. She wrote that by the time she was 15, she had stayed in more than 200 homeless shelters in some 32 states. She said she was virtually illiterate as a result of not having a consistent elementary school education. But through it all, she planned and plotted, knowing she deserved better. Finally, she came up with a scheme. She would get pregnant to emancipate herself so that she could be eligible to apply for benefits and an apartment of her own. She said she made that decision after coming to terms with the fact that her mother, who dragged her from town to town and shelter to shelter, was incapable of caring for her. My point here is not that girls should get pregnant on purpose, or at all for that matter. It's that even when you think there is no way out, where there is a will, there is a way. The key is your belief that you deserve better. By the end of the story, the woman was a single mama; but she was also a homeowner and a college graduate.

It is important for singe mamas to push through all the nonsense and look for ways to build themselves up. Write lists of possibilities and follow through. Take failure and rejection as battle scars, because Sister, you are fighting a war. You are battling for yourself and your kids. Your artillery is love. The beautiful thing about that is that God is love. And God is accessible to all of us. So stop being afraid to succeed.

The cool thing is that if you're reading this book, you already know there's hope. And you want to be a good mother. You're just not sure where to find the tools. So start with what's free, church. O.K., the Bible does mention tithing ten percent of your earnings. But if you ain't got it, you ain't got it. And when you've been going to church for a while, things in your life will start to come together so that lo and behold, one day you will have it. And you'll want to give of your time and talents. Just know that getting to church, finding a really supportive singles ministry or better yet, single mothers' ministry is an important step in the right direction.

Ms Kelly

I used to just move through my life aimlessly. It wasn't until my son was about 4 or 5 years old that I started going to church regularly. I was in Jacksonville, Florida working as a visiting assistant professor and freelance TV news reporter. At the invitation of my friend, Michael Flowers, I discovered a wonderful congregation where the singles ministry offered Bible study classes and events at people's homes where I felt a kind of love I actually did not know existed. It was the kind of love where people really work and demonstrate their desire to be supportive of one another. They worked hard not to curse or gossip or say sarcastic or mean things to one another. When people were broke, others pitched in to help them out. We celebrated one another's victories and prayed for strength with each other when we were feeling weak. All of this rubbed off on me, and as a result, rubbed off on my son.

Winston used to call Wednesday night Bible study at our church, "the Wednesday church party." He called it that because since Bible study was right after work, everyone would stop at the store or a fast food place and bring something; so we'd have a huge potluck while discussing the Bible and sharing how our week had gone so far.

All of this took me away from what I had previously believed was important. I honestly believed a single mama's role in life was to undo her singlehood, to find herself a man. That belief took me places where I had no business, places like clubs bars, and other hangouts, because after all, men were there. Worse, it took me away from where I should have been, at home with my kid.

As single mamas, we should remember that we are mamas first, single second. For our children, if we are the custodial parent, we are our kids' rock. To many, there is no existence without us. They rely on us for everything – their food, clothing, comfort, protection, EVERYTHING. See, to our kids, we represent security. If we are not there, no one is there. They are left insecure to fend for themselves. So above all else, our primary responsibility is to be there for them, not in the streets trying to find some substitute daddy for them. And don't tell me about your best girlfriend who met her husband at a club. There are always exceptions. But we, as single mamas, simply cannot gamble with our time in that way. We don't have that much time. So when we're not working or taking care of our kids, we should spend most of our precious free moments doing something that can be helpful to our families and our individual development as a single mama and a strong, confident woman.

That does not mean your life has to be void of male company or having a good time. It means a single mama cannot be single minded about her pursuit to find a man. It's distracting and for the most part, unproductive.

Focus on your kids; go to their games and school events. Help them with their homework. Take them to the movies and church and on picnics or just to the park to play. Demonstrate that kind of beauty and purpose, and maybe you'll attract someone who wants be a positive addition to your life; and you'll do it without even trying. In the meantime, develop friendships with men – guys who respect you and understand that your priority is your family. Be careful, however. As your relationship with a male friend grows, if you know there is no future for the two of you, do not let your closeness give your kids false hope that they soon will have a stepfather. Also, be careful whom you allow to spend time with your kids. Pedophiles target desperate single mamas as a way to get to their kids. Just as you must watch closely how your female friends behave with your children, you must observe your male friends when they are with the kids.

Something tells me you're not ready for me to leave topic of male company alone, especially because you are sick and tired of feeling lonely. You do not have the patience to wait for Mr. Right. And male friends aren't exactly what you're after. You're looking for Mr. Right Now, Dr. Feelgood.

Ladies, if you think you need a man in your life and you actually believe you have time to sort through the selection process, please try to do it in a way that does not interfere with your family matters. If you believe there will be no overlap, you are so kidding yourself it's not even funny. Courting takes valuable time and attention. Whether you are using an on-line service or dating men you meet at work or at bars, getting to know a guy to figure out whether he is what he says he is takes time away from talking to your kids, tucking them in at night, helping them with their homework, paying attention to caution signs that lead to their getting into trouble, having dinner with them, etc. You should know that going in and ask yourself if Dude is worth it.

I must remind you that if you think the dating game is your only way to find happiness; I believe you're listening to a bunch of hype. I know, I've heard it, myself. I've even acted on it. You believe that you've got to get out and about – without your kids – so that you can just be a woman and attract a man. You have to kiss some frogs to get to your prince and you don't know too many frogs or princes who hang out at your daughter's after-school dance studio. Plus, you can make up lost time with your kids after you find the man of your dreams. Right? Sounds good. But in life there are always tradeoffs.

Single mama, my point is you have to be extra careful when you are bringing anyone into your life. It's a balancing act. No one should come between you and your responsibility to your family.

My advice: if you meet someone who you believe has the qualities of the kind of man you think would make a good husband and stepfather, take your time. Teenagers who get themselves into trouble sexually do so because they are impatient. They are afraid that if they don't give it up, another girl will. Do not be this girl. Know that a man who respects your single mamahood situation will have to suffer a little bit if he is to have you. But that's OK, honey. You're worth it.

And another thing, whatever you do, keep any activity that is even remotely sexual away from your kids. You are a mother and you cannot set examples you do not want your kids to follow. And believe me, if you're bringing guys home, your kids will likely pattern the behavior when they become sexually curious, whether they play the man's role or yours. Plus, please know that no children want to think of their mother as a whore. Oh, yes, that's what I said, ho, whore, whatever. If you're acting like one -- and believe me, to your kids, any casual sexual encounter means you are -- please keep it far away from your children. No guys need to be coming by your house and giving your kids any indication that they know you like that. If that happens, your kids WILL disrespect you. And the sad thing about that is it will be well-earned disrespect, and no one's fault but your own. So please keep your "dating" away from your kids. Please.

I've gotten emails from single mamas who disagree with my tough stance on dating. They think it's good for their kids to see their mothers in healthy relationships. I cannot disagree with that. But ask most single women who are on the dating scene, and they'll tell you most guys they date are not "the one," and too many of their relationships are anything but healthy. That's drama even if you don't have kids. But if you do, and you're bringing your dating drama into your home, you're building hope that will more times than not, prove to be false.

Like you, your kids might like the idea of having a man around. If a guy seems really nice, they may begin to fantasize about him being their stepfather. So what happens if three months into the relationship you learn this guy is eternally unemployed or that he has five kids from five different mothers and he's not taking care of any of them? What if you learn that Mr. Nice Guy is married? What if this happens two or three times in a year? You're heartbroken, right? Well imagine what your kids are going through. I'm giving you tips for keeping it simple -- saving the drama and taking your time without taking your kids through stuff that no kid should have to deal with. That's hard; I know. But no one said being a single mama is easy.

Single mamas, here are some simple rules to follow when it comes to guys in your life:

- **Do NOT have sleepovers when your kids are there, even if there's no sex involved.**
- **As for a guy you believe is "the one," your kids don't need to meet him until after a few months, until you know he's serious. You have to be honest about whether he really would be good for your family. Do not be in denial if he is not. And if he is impatient and leaves, that's your first sign that he does not get your life and probably never will. No worries, if he's the right one, he'll take his time getting to know you first and your children later.**
- **Do not let your guy play step dad with your kids. He does not need to get anywhere near that close to your kids until he's proposed. Even then,**

you be the disciplinarian.

- If your kids are home, meet your dates in a safe place away from home. That way, your kids won't be caught up in your hopes, dreams and/or dating drama.
- Let your kids be kids. Do not share your dating stories with them. Save the drama – if you insist on having it – for their mama.
- Do not let a guy get involved with your family until you have seen enough of his life to believe he will add to, not take from what is positive about your situation.
- Do not be desperate. Having a man just to keep you warm at night is not a good enough reason to have him around.
- Take dating seriously and protect yourself in all ways. If you cannot abstain, please avoid potential infections and pregnancy. It simply is not fair to carelessly bring another child into a single parent-headed home. And don't be naïve enough to think this one will stick around. That's just not the way to catch and keep a man; and you should know this.
- Watch any guy very closely as he's getting to know your kids. Child

predators love to chum up to desperate, lonely single mamas whose kids "need a father figure."

- **Do not leave your young kids alone while you rendezvous with a lover. If something happened to your kids or you, you'd never forgive yourself.**
- **Respect yourself and your family's emotional and physical security. If a man in your life disrupts what's good about your family, he is not worth it.**
- **Do not be in denial; we're talking about your kids here.**

Way Too close for comfort

It never ceases to amaze me how men call radio talk shows where I am the guest who have this "problem" about a single mama situation in which they are involved. The problem usually is shared like this:

"Hello Ms Kelly. My name is Rodney. I'm dating this single mom, and I just can't seem to get her kids to respect me. They also disrespect her in front of me, and she won't let me discipline them."

And my response:

"Yes, and what's your question."

"What can I do to get the kids to respect their mother and me? Also, what can I do to get my lady to let me discipline the kids?"

That's where I have to tell the caller what he doesn't expect and certainly does not want to hear.

"Well, Rodney, how long have you been seeing her? And why do you think the kids should respect you?"

"I've been seeing their mom six weeks. They should respect me," he goes on, "because I am an adult and a father figure to them. Their own daddies are never around and hardly pay child support."

And then Ms. Kelly has to say something like this.

"Rodney, here's the deal. You say you're a father figure. Does that mean you sleep in the home with the kids' mom?"

"Yes," he says.

"Well, Rodney, the kids know that. They are not stupid. As they see it, you're basically violating their family life as it was; you're in essence, keeping them from their mother and doing who knows what with her at night behind closed doors. They see you eating their food and taking their mother away. And you're claiming the role of their daddy when they already have one, even if *you* don't see it that way.

Give me a reason why the kids should respect you. And before you do that, think about this. What if you were one of those kids? What if your lady was your mother and you were the kid? Would you respect you? You have no right to discipline those kids; they don't even know you.

And if your lady really wants her kids to respect her, she needs to slow down with you. See you when it's not on her kids' time. She should only let them have to deal with the fact that their mama is sleeping with someone when you've walked her down the aisle and put a ring on her finger. That's when you will have earned their respect.

Single mamas, let your love interest know that he'd better be ready for the big time. Only the strong survive. Trust me, that's one of the reasons second marriages fail more often than the first ones. And single mama, that's why you're really better off doing your thing with everything you have, all your energies. Do the mama thing right and if it's meant to be, the right man will go through the proper motions or wait till your babies are out of the house or at least away at their daddy's house for the summer.

There's one more thing to consider here, too. There might be a reason that you are not supposed to have a man in your life right now. Maybe you're not ready for your soul mate. Maybe he's out there getting ready for you. The wrong relationship can make you miss your blessing.

Things happen for a reason, so if it doesn't feel right to you or your children, something very well could be wrong. In any event, you need to take your time before you take a major step that even in the best of circumstances could change everything your kids see as normal, safe and secure.

Bottom line; do surround yourself with people – friends, family and colleagues – who support your efforts to be the best mama you can be. That goes for the women and men in your life.

3

Don't Hate on Your Kids' Daddy; And Please, No "Baby's Mama Drama."

O.K., you might be wondering, what is this Ms. Kelly talking about, "Let your kids love their daddy?" She obviously doesn't know my kids' daddy. Well you're right, Mama. But guess what? It doesn't matter. Even if I did know him, I would not be able to change him. Once you figure out that you can't change the guy either, you're on your way to reducing the drama for your favorite single mama. So pay attention while I explain.

Every time I do a workshop or a discussion with single mamas, I hear about all the daddy drama. The stories are as unique as the women who share them. But there are similarities.

This is not to minimize what you're going through, but the stories pretty much fall into three categories: the absent daddy, the irresponsible daddy and the controlling daddy. Let me try to explain to you what I've learned about each of these general groupings of guys. Then I'll get into the "Let your kids love their daddy" details. Finally, we'll deal with the grouping that many fortunate single mamas will recognize, the good daddy who does his best. And we'll hope that all the other baby's daddies who happen to be reading this book will find a way to qualify for that category.

By the way, ladies, and not to get negative, but please note that there are exceptions to the let their kids see their daddy situation. We're talking about letting them love their daddy, which you should do no matter what. But in cases where the dad is a known, convicted child predator or abuser of some sort, I do not advocate that you subject your kids to any dangerous situations or people, not even their dad. While I know cases like these are rare, I would be remiss in not addressing them. In those cases, you must simply be honest with your kids. Tell them the good things they're longing to hear about their dad, as long as they're true. But also tell them he did something very wrong to hurt a child (or adult, whatever the facts of the story), and that you do not trust him around them. Tell them you want to protect them from any behavior that might harm them.

The absent daddy

The absent father is a fact of life for many single mamas. Widows face the issue for obvious reasons. Then there are women whose children's fathers are away because of military or other work assignments. Other daddies are incarcerated. But most single mama drama issues surround the absent daddy who almost never comes around for reasons unknown to the single mama. Herein lies the heartache.

I raise the issue of widows and the mamas whose children's fathers are away at work or locked up because there are lessons to be learned from these mamas. For the most part, I've found that these mothers accept their situations in ways that reduce their "absent daddy" drama. I've found that many of these mamas' children have photographs of their daddies in their bedrooms; they talk about their fathers and cherish the few instances that they recall spending time with them.

As we explore the general category of the absent daddy and the drama associated, we should keep these mamas in mind and learn from them.

The absent daddy I hear most about is the guy who may have been there for you during your pregnancy and even shortly after the baby was born. But then you started seeing less and less of him. He lost interest in you, and with that came less interest in his baby. When you really think about it, he really wasn't around a whole lot even before you got pregnant, let alone during the pregnancy and now. Sure, he may have talked a good game and even delivered sometimes with cash money and gifts, diapers and high chairs and stuff. But his visits were always short. He always seemed distracted and acted like he would rather be somewhere else.

This absent daddy likely has other kids he never sees. Sadly, you knew this when you got involved with him. Back then, you referred to his baby's mama's (or mamas') constant calls and badmouthing as "baby's mama drama." But look who has the drama now.

Come on Sister. No offense, but did you really expect this smooth talking hustler to change? O.K., forgive me. So he's not a hustler. He's a professional man. Regardless, you saw the signs. If you're honest, you'll see that you may have even enabled his bad behavior.

Have you gone after child support? I don't mean have you called him up and told him off. I mean did you go to your local child support enforcement office? What are you afraid of? What? You think if you file for child support, he won't come around? Give me a break. Chances are if he has to pay, he'll actually demand that he see his kids. If he's so angry that he stays away, that's on him, not you. The only thing you might be able to control here is taking every step you can to give your child support from both parents. Your children deserve to be able to know their father. They also deserve to be provided for by him.

Ladies, you cannot control whether a man is going to come and see his baby. But there are laws that allow you to at least do everything in your power to get him to live up to at least one part of his responsibility. The first thing a good single mama does is to make sure she provides for her kids. She puts them in the safest home she can afford; provides them with healthy meals, and dresses them in clean, appropriate, neat clothing. You might be able to do it by yourself. But believe me, you can do more for them if their daddy pitches in. And at least you can tell them he's helping.

But, regardless of whether he's paying, the lesson you should take from this book is simple. Do not let your anger be one more reason he stays away. Children remember those few times with their fathers and carry those moments in their hearts. Your negativity can taint those precious moments. Those rare visits might be your kids' tiny reminder that despite their father's issues, they have his love. While he is out there deciding what he's going to do about his life or maybe not even thinking about his kids, do not make any rules, even to yourself, about how he will never see his kids, even if he comes back crawling. Don't let you and your pride be one more excuse. Trust me, this guy has enough of his own.

A Daddy and His Daughter

One time, while I was doing a parent education class in Chicago, the only dad who showed up actually admitted that he was one of those absentee or "deadbeat" dads. It was hard, I could only imagine, but he confessed right there in front of a room full of single mamas.

"I really want to do better," he said. "But I'm scared my baby's mama won't believe me. The more time that passes, the harder it gets. I know she doesn't trust me."

This man, who had not seen his teenaged daughter since she was about four, said he used to write his baby's mama checks. After he started seeing another woman, she became very angry with him and told him she never wanted him around her daughter.

Over the years, he often thought of his daughter. There were times when he made enough money to really help out; but he didn't want to just give his ex money without being able to see his child. At least that's how he justified it.

I told him to imagine what his daughter must think – that she probably has heard nothing about him over the years except the bad stuff. I told him that his daughter's mama had probably forgotten all the reasons she had fallen for him so many years ago. I told him the anger had probably mounted with each day that passed, every week, month and year that went by when she had not heard from him. There was no way, I told him, that his daughter had not heard those bad things and held onto them. Why shouldn't she have, I asked him. She had no proof, no reason to believe anything else.

But I also told him the younger children are, the more likely they are to hold onto hope. Every kid I know wants both parents. Sometimes they pretend they don't as a way of protecting themselves and so as not to feel foolish for believing in fairy tales that day after day, week after week, month after month, never come true.

I told this daddy that the more time that goes by, the more difficult it's going to be, so don't let another day go by. I suggested he write to the mom, send her some money and beg for forgiveness and permission to see his daughter. I also told him to tell the mother the truth – that he is grateful that she's been keeping it together and giving his daughter what he had not. I told him to try everything he could, even to go to court and establish a child support schedule and some kind of visitation, even if only supervised. It had a chance of failing, but the more sincere he was, the better his chances of being successful. I told him to earn some trust and to understand his daughter's potential pain and mistrust. Years had destroyed what he was trying to rebuild. But he'd have to be patient because that's a quality of a good parent. We'll do what it takes to build up our kids. We do it because we love them, patiently and kindly.

Mama, my lesson to you in all of this is that with all those passing years, the daughter in this story is likely to feel her daddy's absence in ways she doesn't even know. She is likely to look elsewhere for the approval she would have gotten from her daddy. Often teenagers, tempted to test their sexual limitations anyway, are needy in all kinds of ways. They're often insecure. Even the most beautiful girls feel awkward and goofy and out of place at some point in their lives, usually starting at about age 11 or 12. Without a father around to tell her that she's smart and pretty and that she is too good to be giving herself to just any boy at any time, the temptation can be way too much. It's no wonder so many 14 and 15-year-old girls will do anything to hear a boy say she's fine or sexy or beautiful. Sometimes, just to hear someone of the opposite sex say something to her that she never hears is enough to make her do anything to hear it again. A girl needs to know her father loves her. Please, Mama, I repeat, don't be the one to stand in her way.

Do whatever you can to let your kids love even the memory of their absentee daddy. When they ask about him, think of everything you possibly can that is or was good about him, and share it with him. Is he tall or handsome? Is he smart and funny? What was it about him that you were attracted to? Whatever it was, you'd better keep your pride and anger to yourself and share it when your kids ask. If they ask you why he's not around, tell them the truth. You don't know. But tell them one thing you do know is that it has absolutely nothing to do with them. After all, he doesn't even know them. Tell them how sorry you are that he's missing all these great years. If possible, let your kids spend time with his family so that at least they get to experience their father in some way. Your kids will always have an emptiness and a strange sense of loss and longing for their father. Do what you can to fill the void with positive stories. And when he does come around, step out of the way and let the visit take its course. Then thank Papa for coming around and tell him what it meant to your children. Positive reinforcement may not work miracles, but it offers the only thing you have when the absentee daddy finally does show up – hope that he'll keep it up.

The irresponsible daddy

I think this is the daddy I hear the most about. This is the daddy who grates on the single mama's nerves, not because she hates you, but because she has to do some much extra work because of you. There was a reason you were attracted to her and vice versa. You needed a mama and maybe back then, she needed someone to take care of. Well now she has a real child, so your boyish ways aren't so charming anymore.

These are usually the guys who mean well, but are so busy spreading their love and joy, that it's hard for them to keep their word let alone keep up with those to whom they gave it. For whatever reasons, these guys attract women who are exactly their opposite.

The irresponsible daddy is usually described to me in my workshops by a mother who is pretty much a perfectionist. I don't mean this in a negative way either. She at some point was truly this man's better half. These are the mamas who really take care of business, the ones who do what they say they're going to do, pay their bills on time, keep their kids on a schedule and make sure they do their homework. These are the mamas who cannot tolerate people who say they're going to do something and end up not doing it. She gets very protective of her children when her kids' daddy makes promises that he does not keep.

The frustration becomes even more intense because this mama does not know how to handle all the missed or late or changed-at-the-last-minute appointments.

By now you should know that I always preach to single mamas that they should try to layoff on dating until after they've done all they can to get their kids through their early years, on a path of independence and at least halfway out of the house. I did this, myself (well, OK, there were a few exceptions, those that gave me enough experience on this matter to feel strongly about it). For the most part, I put off dating until after Winston left for school.

By that time, I found it was hard for me to date any guy who had kids without constantly telling him what he could probably do better to help his baby's mama. Perhaps not ironically, for a number of reasons previously mentioned, the first guy I actually fell for ended up being one of these "irresponsible daddy" types.

Let's call him, "Carl"

I saw Carl across the room at a party, and he was about as cute as they come. (Later I discovered he was also as slick as they come. But we'll get there.)   Our eyes met, then we met, flirted and exchanged numbers. The next thing you know, we were dating. Carl was transitioning into a second career when I met him. So he was pretty busy and had little free time. (But men make time for what's important to them. We do, too.)

On our first date, I told Carl about Winston, who was away at school, and he told me about his son. Later that week, he e-mailed me a photo of the little boy. The child, then two years old, lived in a nearby town with his mom, who is an attractive (she was in the photo, too) professional woman. From what I gathered, she seemed smart and had her stuff together. But when Carl talked about his baby's mama, he was usually complaining about her attempts to get more child support or get him to visit his baby more. He said she nagged him when he was late or had a change of plans.

Carl had no idea who he was talking to. But after I lectured him about the fact that his baby's mama was right and that his little boy needed his daddy and that his constant changes of plans were not good for the kid or for his relationship with the boy's mama, he did start to see things a little clearer. He seemed to be having his son in town with him more and I noticed a friendlier tone when he'd talk to his baby's mama.

Carl had a lot of issues with his own daddy. He was one of those "outside" kids, the ones the daddy has on the side, outside of his marriage. Often the people in these daddies' churches and professions have no idea about their love children. This was the case with Carl's father and it bothered my friend to no end. He was angry and sad. Even as a grown man, he was trying to win his daddy's approval and love. I believed this had a lot to do with Carl's own tentative relationship with his own little boy, and I gently pointed it out to him on more than one occasion.

Eventually, I found out Carl had more problems than I even imagined. I discovered he was cheating on me with a woman who lived in my building; he actually knew her first and was crazy about her, but she had previously dumped him and was sometimes letting him back in. It was during that period that I discovered what was going on.

Despite how much Carl had told me about the pain his own dad caused him and his mom, he hurt his baby's mama in similar ways and sometimes found himself acting irresponsibly by not keeping his word with his son. And what his dad did to his wife was exactly what Carl was doing to me, the woman downstairs, and who knows whom else he was messing around with. Also like his own father, Carl was selfish and bold enough to do it in a way where he would and did get caught.

I'm not sure if Carl ever worked it out with his baby's mama. My fear is that his inconsistency and bad habits continue to this day.

Ladies, if you are the mama of a child whose daddy is irresponsible, there's really nothing you can do to change the guy. Even Ms. Kelly couldn't change Carl and he wasn't even her baby's daddy! But one thing you can do to keep your sanity is change your reaction to this kind of daddy's selfish ways and adjust your expectations as well. (When I think back, I recall Carl telling me to lower my expectations with him; I should have listened.)

In other words, do not even tell your kids when daddy's planning to pick them up. Let them do their regular thing and only when you know for sure he's coming, then tell them or call them at their friend's house down the street to let them know Daddy's on his way. While this might be annoying to the kids, they'll forget all about not being able to hang out with their friends when their daddy comes. Or, they might even want their daddy to meet their friends. In other words, since this "irresponsible" baby's daddy is so spontaneous, you and your kids should be the same way. This will save you and the kids so much heartache and you'll be far less stressed out about the situation.

I know this sounds crazy, far-fetched and just awkward, but if you keep doing the same thing, you'll have the same stressful results. Change it up a bit and you and your kids can be a lot happier. By the way, if your kids ask why you didn't tell them Daddy was coming before he showed up, tell them you didn't know for sure and didn't want to get their hopes up. The truth shall set you free, my dear!

The controlling daddy

Last year, at one of my Black Star Parent University workshops, I met Dawn, a single mama who told me that her baby's daddy pays regular child support and sees his son every summer. She said he saw her son more than that before she moved to Chicago from Florida, where this daddy lives. But Dawn said her only problem was that her ex was so controlling.

Dawn described how her son's father, a Nigerian-American college professor, was still angry five years after her breakup. She said the breakup was the result of the fact that she had grown up a lot since marrying her son's father five years prior to her baby's birth. She said back then, when her husband said he expected her to stay home, not work and that her only jobs would be to care for his home and him, she thought that was wonderful.

However, as Dawn got older (she was 22 and he was nearly 40 when they met), what appeared to her to be rigid African rules and traditions were things with which she could no longer live. She felt imprisoned and wanted out. By then, however, she and her husband had a son, whom I'll call Alex.

Breaking up with her husband and going through a divorce was extremely difficult. Her husband was deeply hurt and offended that the woman he married turned out to be a totally different person. She had even begun going on weekend trips with her girlfriends and spending time in the evenings at clubs and bars. He could not imagine that this woman would be responsible for mothering his son, who at the time of the divorce was 12.

During their separation and even after they divorced, Dawn said she began to feel that Alex's father was having her followed. She said whenever he would come to pick up his son, he asked the boy personal questions about his mother's life, insisting that she was seeing someone and threatening to fight her for custody if, in fact, she was. She said Alex told her that his daddy spent most of their time together asking him about his mama.

On top of all of this, Dawn said her ex would often cut short weekends and even one-day outings with their son only to show up early at her house and wait until she got home. He'd argue with her in front of her son, accusing her of not caring to wait at home for her son and calling her a bad mother. This went on for two years.

Finally, when Dawn got the opportunity for a promotion and an out-of-state job transfer, she jumped at the chance to be free. Her ex tried to stop the move legally; but he now had a girlfriend who encouraged him to stop fighting it. Dawn and her ex agreed to have Alex spend summers in Florida.

Still, Dawn said her son's father was threatening to follow through on what he'd said so many times earlier about pursuing primary custody. She also was afraid that when her son went to be with his father for the summer, her ex would persuade Alex to ask his mom if he could stay after the summer and live with his dad.

By now, Alex was 14. I asked her if she thought he wanted to live with his father. She said sometimes he did. I asked how she thought that might work out, her feelings aside. She smiled and took a while to answer. Since we were in a group, I told her to give me her answer after the workshop.

Later, Dawn told me her son often spoke of wanting to live with his father – particularly when she was traveling a lot for work or hanging out a lot with her friends. I asked her to be honest with herself and me and tell me whether she thinks it might be time to let go – to let Alex live with his dad. I told her that at 14, if Alex changed his mind and wanted to return to Chicago, it would be difficult for his father to force him to stay, particularly since she had legal physical custody. I also told her that in my experience, many kids who suddenly begin living with the non-custodial parent have such a tough time adjusting, that they want to go back to the home with which they are most familiar.

I asked Dawn if she believes despite his overbearing and controlling ways with her, that Alex's father was a good dad. She said she does and that, in fact, since he started seeing his girlfriend, he'd chilled on his obsession with Dawn.

Then I asked her why she's hanging on, why *she's* being so controlling (I asked her this with a smile), in terms of having her son live with her when it might be time to try letting him live with his dad. I told her that she appears to want to have everything her way; she wants to party and have her son with her, despite what her son and her ex are saying they want. I told her she might want to consider giving everyone what they want right now. Maybe after a trial period, everyone would find this was in Alex's best interest. If not, at least she would know she did not stand in the way of giving it a try.

*I believe everyone's situation is different. However, when children, particularly boys, express interest in living with their dads – and their dads are willing, able and capable of handling the responsibility, this is something you should explore. He may have as much right as you do to have custody. On the other hand, if you feel that a father's "controlling" is in any way dangerous – if you, for example, believe the father would kidnap the children and take them to another country – get legal help and advice. (This so rarely happens that it should not be an issue. But I bring it up because there are exceptions to all this single mama's dos and don'ts.)

More on the exceptions to a single mama's dos and don'ts

*Please note, ladies, I cannot reiterate enough that there are exceptions to all my dos and don'ts. When it comes to our babies' daddies, the biggest exception to my rules comes with the abusive daddy. If your child's father is a man who has abused you or your children or has threatened to do so, he needs

help and you need professional intervention for your safety and your kids'. No one should be subjected to abuse. If you need a safe place to go to get away from an abuser, get in touch with law enforcement right away and let them connect you with the resources you need. Do not try to be the savior for this man, no matter how much you love him. You are not God; you are a human being. This man needs help that you are incapable of providing. All you can do is protect yourself and your kids and pray for their daddy. You cannot fix him.

The good daddy

I leave the best for last. Children of many single mamas have good daddies, but you wouldn't know this by what we read in the papers and see on T.V. In fact, I believe we single mamas buy the hype so much that even if our baby's daddy is a good father, we are so busy focusing on the negatives that we don't see it.

Kendra

Case in point, Kendra. Kendra married her son's father two years after the baby was born. Kendra got pregnant about 8 months after she and Andre met at a popular dance club in Tampa. Kendra had already had two abortions and there was no way she was going to go through another one. (She was actually on the pill this time, but she got careless and started taking it off schedule and sometimes even missed pills.)

Two days before Kendra's wedding, she had a case of frozen feet. She was scared to death and wanted to call the whole thing off. It wasn't that she had any particular issue with her baby's father. It's just that she felt she wasn't really in love and that the only reason she was marrying him was because he was her son's daddy.

Like all friends who don't know any better (and some who do), we were so preoccupied with the wedding and with what we thought was best for Kendra and her son, Steffan, that we encouraged her to go through with it. As bridesmaids, her best girlfriends, myself included, went with her to the cake tasting, florist, caterer – you name it. We were so caught up in the wedding that we didn't stop to think about what would happen after all the pomp and circumstance were over. We never thought about what would happen later, after more kids when Kendra would wake up and wonder what she'd gotten herself into.

So about ten years after her wedding, with three young kids, Kendra went through the difficult steps of first informing her kids' daddy that she wanted a divorce and then going through all of the ugly painful steps – the give and take, arguing, second guessing, crying, accusing, shouting, the entire heart-wrenching process.

It has been a year since the divorce became final. Andre is still a bit shell shocked, but he has finally accepted that things are what they are.

Kendra is happier and has met a man she believes is her soul mate (even though he's married). At the same time, she struggles with the issues of being a divorced mother. She feels she never gets enough financial support from Andre. And she becomes completely livid when he has his girlfriend at his house when the kids are there for a visit.

But the fact is, Andre pays what the court has ordered. He does a lot of other extras as well, never letting the fact that he pays child support get in the way of his buying the kids what they want, if he can afford it, when he is with them. He also chose to live close to Kendra and the kids. Despite the fact that he did not want the divorce, he spends four out of seven days a week with his children.

Our babies' daddies are not perfect and neither are we

What we really need to do as single mamas is to remember that just as we are not perfect, neither are our babies' daddies. That, alone, does not make them poor fathers. But we also need to understand that we have to be bigger than our anger and our longing for him (if that's an issue) so that no matter what, we are putting our children first. This is not about us, Mamas; it's about our babies. And we want our kids to have every possible opportunity to succeed in life, to respect themselves, to love and to be happy, safe and secure.

Tips for dealing with your babies' daddy (or daddies):

- **Give them the benefit of the doubt**

- **Give them positive reinforcement when they keep their word**

- **Let them know how much their kids love them and depend on them for their well being**

- **Tell them how you and the kids feel about what he does right as well as what he does wrong, but do not share your disappointing feelings with him in the kids' presence**

- **Follow through on efforts to collect child support, even if he threatens not to see the kids if he has to pay; a man who wants to see his kids will let nothing get in the way**

- **Let your children talk about their fathers, wish for them, put photos of them in their rooms and anything else that demonstrates love for them.**

- If your children ask why their fathers do not see them more, tell them the truth -- that you really don't know. But let them know what you do know for sure, that it has absolutely nothing to do with the child. Let them know that sometimes adults get wrapped up in things that keep them busy and that you are sorry their father is missing a chance to get to watch his daughter or son grow up, because it's a wonderful opportunity and they are great kids.

- Accept that you cannot control another human being. But you can control your own reaction to that person's behavior.

- If you are going back and forth with your child's father, stop. If he does not want to commit to you, stop kidding yourself. End the relationship and stick to your guns. No spending the night because his kid asked him to, none of that. Flip the script so that it is clear that his relationship is with his child, not with you. If that means he stops coming around for a while, so be it. If he's a good father, he'll get over the rejection and resume his relationship with his child. Other men do it and he can, too.

4

Do Not Overspend.

Many single mamas I know struggle with money. That's despite whether they are on the low or medium end of the economic spectrum. One of the reasons is single mama guilt.

When I ask single mothers about overspending, many admit that they do not hesitate to indulge their children. Many single mamas say they want to try to get their kids what they didn't have when they were younger.

Whenever I really break this down, however, the guilt over being a single mama comes up. Thinking you can make up for what your kids do not have in terms of a traditional family, in my opinion, is at the heart of the problem with many a single mama and her financial woes. She is, in many ways trying to compensate for not having a husband.

My sister friend

A very close and dear friend of mine who is currently unemployed called me yesterday to tell me that in the wee hours of the morning, someone with a tow truck quietly took her car from her driveway. She knew it was coming.

For many single mamas, managing money is a foreign concept. Many work in low-income jobs, and live at the poverty level. Others who make decent money often live beyond their means. People give me a hard time for being cheap, for always living under my income level. I do this for two reasons. For one, I never know when I might be out of work. Second, I want to teach my son not to expect to get everything he wants. I want him to see all the hard work that goes into getting "things." I spent a lot of his childhood preaching about how people can get blinded and tempted when they are impressed with material goods rather than a person's character -- the Christ-like qualities that we, as Christians, should admire, that Godly or spiritual people should strive to have.

So, you might be wondering, how does that goody-two-shoes values position translate into tips that would keep an unemployed single mama from having her car repossessed? There are always financial crises that cannot be helped. Anyone who lived in the Gulf region during

Hurricane Katrina knows that. But there are always ways we can be ready when hard times hit.

My friend, whom I'll call Brenda, and I discussed the kinds of things that put us in the squeezes that keep us from having enough money to pay our bills when we face a crisis. She admitted to something about her situation that gives us all an important lesson. (I had told her she might consider not worrying about getting the car back and paying two years of payments with interest. I thought she should take a friend up on her offer to let her drive a car she doesn't use and wait a few months to pay cash for a used car.) What she said took a lot of courage. She said she was worried about what people might say.

When Brenda shared this with me, I told her I was proud of her for admitting it. (She knows how "naggy" I can be about the issue of overspending.) I also told her to please not worry about other people, that she is a single mama with two kids holding down a mortgage payment. Many of her neighbors are probably also faking the funk, pretending they can afford to live a lot larger than they really can as well. There's no shame in admitting that you are cutting costs to save money. That's something few families have the willpower or discipline to do. If your neighbors don't understand, so be it. They're not doing anything for you or your kids anyway.

I suggested to her that rather than collect more than $2,000, robbing Peter to Pay Paul and the tow truck company and bank, she should not try to get the car back. She should just let them have the car and let the loan go into collections.

She said she was worried about her credit. I told her that she just bought a house and that the reason people try to have a good credit score is usually so that they can buy a house. Keeping her house is more important than keeping a car. She can always rebuild her credit rating after the car setback. That car and its way too large payments were not worth her losing her new house.

I suggested that she should instead, save the $500 per month car payment, or whatever she can afford, and buy a used car for under $5,000 in a few months. She lives in a city where you can buy a decent used car for $3,500. I live in Chicago and bought a used 1997 Jeep last year for about $5,000 and have had no real problems with it. I did that because at the time, I had $5,000 in cash. I also had a decent-paying job and could have financed a fancier new car, but I'm not trying to impress anyone. And I never want to be in a situation where I'm out of work and have more to pay than my mortgage payment.

The point is you never know what's coming. If you want to be true to yourself and your kids, you have to teach them to reject all the hype, all the messages in rap songs and movies and everything around them that would have them believe their value is tied to brand name clothing, jewelry and other material things. We have to teach our kids that freedom is being able to walk away from a job, even if it's with a pink slip, and know that for a while, what's in the bank will take care of our bills. Our bills have to be kept to a minimum so that the first bill we pay is always to our own savings account.

Clearly no one can live in this country without in some way being impacted by all the materialism. There are ways to treat ourselves and our kids to some of the finer things in life without spending more than we have.

When I was a little girl, my mother taught me to always go to the back of stores. That's usually where you'll find the items on clearance. Discount stores like Wal-Mart and Target also have some choice items for good prices. I should also mention that while I get lot of compliments on my clothing and consider myself a pretty good dresser, many of my better outfits include at least one item that came from a thrift store. (I've had larger women tell me that's because I never have to get anything bigger than a size 8, and smaller sizes are easier to find at these places. While I agree that most of the nicer items are smaller sizes, I've seen good quality larger items as well.) There is no shame in saving money and no prestige in buying bling labels just because you saw or heard about them on a music video or in your favorite fashion magazine. And of course a lot of single mamas know about Marshall's and TJ Maxx. They are a great way to get a deal on the better brands. We just have to stay out of the stores when we don't have money.

No means Mama doesn't have it

But what about your kids, you ask? Kids want so much. They go to school and see what the other kids have and insist that they'll be losers if they don't also have it. This is where you have to remember that you are the boss. No matter how sulky or angry your kids get when you say, "no," they'll eventually get over it or find a way to earn it. The kid benefits either way.

What you should do is teach your kids how to stretch a dollar. Try not to finance anything that you can get by waiting a month and paying cash, no matter how many offers you get in the mail or from the sales clerk. With items for your home, you can always buy used stuff. The house I own is a two-flat. I have tenants in one of the units and we share the washer and dryer. Last week, the dryer broke. I went to Home Depot to see what they had on sale. The lowest priced gas dryer was one on clearance for about $260. With delivery, installation and tax, I would have been out of more than $350. (In fairness, there was a delivery rebate for $50, but I'd have to wait to get that in the mail.)

So I went home and went onto my computer and typed in www.craigslist.org. I scrolled down the For Sale area and sure enough, I saw a two-year-old Maytag dryer for $100. I called a friend with a van and it was in my basement drying my tenants' clothes the next evening.

You should consider buying items for your home from garage sales and thrift shops. Not only is this fun and a good way to teach your kids how to bargain, it allows you to buy unique, higher-quality items. Your house will not look like everyone else's. It will look better. Watch HGTV and you'll see how they make treasure out of trash. They do not think mass produced furniture sets are cool. They're just too cookie cutter. And they really cost more than they are worth.

I should mention that my friend, Brenda, had been paying $500 a month to rent a dining room set. You can buy a beautiful used dining room set from people who are moving for a couple hundred bucks. You might even get lucky and find a great antique. (Brenda did return the rental furniture as a first cost-cutting move.)

Just be patient, save and when you do shop, do not rule out the garage sales and thrift shops.

Oh, and before you do that, ask people you know who have furniture stacked in their garage if you can help them take it off their hands. Don't be proud. While there are plenty of greedy people who'll try to charge you too much for stuff no one is even using, there are others who are generous and kind who'll be happy to give you things for little or nothing. Just ask around at work and church. You'll see.

Are you in a bind or always broke?
Here are some tips on saving
and managing money:

- Ask whether daycare or after-school care charges are based on a sliding scale. If so, apply for reduced prices. That's what it's there for.

- Cook at home as much as possible

- If you do not qualify for a reduced-price school lunch plan, make lunch or pack leftovers for you and your kids

- Limit treats like desserts and alcohol to once a week

- Do not rent furniture or appliances. Do without them -- yes even a TV, until you have the money. Or ask around to see if you have family or friends who have these things stored away somewhere. Many people are happy to donate to help a single mama out.

- Pay cash for used stuff. People are always trying to get rid of furniture, dishes, appliances and other household items.   Check out estate sales, garage sales and thrift shops.

- Stop trying to impress people with your big TV, fancy car or designer clothes. Many people go into debt to impress people they don't even like. Only buy what you can afford.

- Try not to finance used cars. If you have no cash and have to get one on credit, try to buy it from a family member who won't charge you interest.

- If you can, take the bus until you can save enough to buy a car for cash; for example, save that $350 a month for 8-12 months, and you can get a decent used car for cash.

- Take advantage of any low-income housing that you can get. Sometimes cities require developers to reserve some otherwise high-income apartments for low-income people. Ask around.

- For birthday gifts for your kids' friends and decorations for parties and kitchen items and all kinds of other things that come up, go to your neighborhood Family Dollar store.

- Do not break your neck and pocketbook to get your kids everything they want.

You'll only spoil them for the real world, which will teach them that it isn't that easy -- you have to work to get what you want. And most of what you think you want, you really don't need.

- Have a side gig. Do you sew or bake great cakes or write poetry or braid hair? Then let your neighbors know and get your hustle on. It's a good way to keep a little cash on hand for emergencies. It might even lead to a successful entrepreneurial venture. Embrace your God-given gifts and talents and put them to work.

- Stop tripping off of other people. You set your own standards. Do not overspend to live the lie that you have more than you do. People impressed by that kind of thing are the kinds of people single mamas need to keep at arm's length.

Put your money on the good stuff

Perhaps the most important thing a single mama can do to help manage her money is to know that the best thing you can give your kids is something that costs nothing. It's your time and the sharing of your values, demonstrated by your financial self-discipline.

One of my favorite movies in the world is *Willy Wonka and the Chocolate Factory* and the remake, *Charlie and the Chocolate Factory*. Have you ever seen it? If not, rent it and watch it with your kids over and over again. Try to get the older ones to watch it with you as well. They'll probably be happy to spend the quality time with you and be surprised that you want to watch a kids' movie.

That movie is so beautiful and has many life's lessons. Any kid who does not walk away from that movie at least a little better is, as Willy might say, simply "rotten." Charlie was such a sweet kid who came from a very poor, very strong family. Family included grandparents and other extended relatives. Everyone took care of everyone. Their wealth was in a good, hot meal, where everyone supported each other's dreams and appreciated what they had, not what they did not have.

Love doesn't cost a thing

I wish we could learn to value love like that again in our communities. I think it's what kids really want. If you talk to little kids about whether they are happy and why, they'll tell you things that might surprise you. Ask them if they had a good day at school, for example. If they say yes, ask them why. They'll say things like, "My teacher smiled at me." Or "Michael played with me." Or "Tiffany said hi to me."

Sure, kids get excited about new toys and new dresses and new shoes. But if you overdo it, they'll come to expect it. And you'll be breaking your neck to spoil them. They'll never learn the value of working hard and saving and waiting and sharing. Those are the qualities that make for a good kid and, later, a great adult. So give your kids some of that stuff. Again, if they get mad, they'll get over it. If they compare themselves, tell them over and over that they'll appreciate it later and that they should work hard and make good grades and they'll have won the race, just like in the story of the Tortoise and the Hare. I know all this sounds simple and corny. But it works.

I found that my son is more compassionate and understanding when I have to tell him, "No" or "Wait." It drives him to work harder to make his own money (even though he knows I'd rather have him just focus on school and getting through college).

The fact is Winston knows I love him. While he usually gets what he wants, he understands I cannot do everything I'd like for him. Above all, he appreciates that I'm just one mama doing my best.

5

Do Instill Self Discipline.

Understanding how to get your kids to be self-disciplined is something most of us learn on the job of being a single mama. In too many cases, unfortunately, the lesson goes unlearned until it's too late.

When people ask me about discipline, they're usually thinking about the rod – whether you should spare it and send your kids to time out or beat your kids into submission. So let me tell you my feelings on corporal punishment, then we'll take a look at discipline.

In my opinion, you should not spare the rod, but nor should you look at a rod as a tool with which to beat your children. Rather, I believe a single mama should use the rod to strictly enforce rules and regulations, consistently and patiently using it for pointing and leading her children in the right direction. That use of the rod, I believe leads to self-discipline.

Among the definitions of discipline are that it is "training" that develops "self control," "character" or "orderliness" and "efficiency." It is defined as "strict control" to "enforce obedience" and a "system of rules."

Discipline takes time, attention and thought. It's a process of teaching a child to have self-control.

Spanking and whipping usually takes anger and force and only a few moments. The feeling behind it can be heat-of-the-moment anger or premeditated. That is my definition of abuse, not discipline. Sure, there are some kind souls who have been known to restrain themselves, giving kids a one or two-swat controlled paddling or switching. But that's still not my idea of discipline. It's just making a point. I believe in many cases, it also terrorizes children and/or turns them into sneaks.

I was recently a guest on Rolonda Watts' "Ro Show," her new radio program. The topic was just this issue – "to spank or not to spank." While Ro said she is not in favor of spanking, she mentioned a report that found many chief executive officers got spanked when they were children. I pointed out that while that might be true, huge percentages of children who are in juvenile detention say they, too, got spanked (or beaten).

A single mama has to be the queen disciplinarian. She has to instill values in her children that train them into being self-controlled adults who want to be good people, not to avoid punishment, but in order to feel good about themselves. That kind of discipline takes intelligence and the kind of patience of which love is made.

Before I launch into my philosophy about discipline, let me say that I have spanked my kid. In the few instances that I can recall, I, like so many parents who beat their kids, was angry and had lost control. I'd had it up to here (way up there). Sound familiar? One of the side effects of being an outspoken parent is having a mouthy child; and I confess, sometimes I was not patient or clever enough to think of more appropriate correction. (The last time I hit Winston was when he was in middle school. He was sassing me and I slapped him. And the slap was somewhat premeditated, too.) I know and knew I was wrong.

All kids are different, but I think patterns that establish that you are the mother and they are the children are far more effective than whippings. Plus, when the kids get older and bigger than you, if force is your only means of discipline, you're going to be in trouble, Mama.

The word discipline and Disciple are related. Both involve having a teacher or a role model. Mama, when it comes to your kids' role model, tag, you're it.

If you instill discipline in your children, you will increase the odds that they will feel safe and protected and will be motivated to do their best, even when you are not around.

If you're a single mama, know that even if your child is older, you can still become a disciplinarian. It starts with knowing and believing that you are the boss. No matter how much your kids cry, whine and complain, guess what? They can't do a thing about it, because you are the queen of your castle. And when it all comes down to it, the kids need you more than they do anything or anyone else.

When I was a pre-teen and my mother married Dr Leon Kelley, a San Diego pediatrician, I gained three stepbrothers. At the time, my mom had four children -- older sister, my younger brother, younger sister and myself. (My mom's story is a whole other book, which I will be honored to write once she grants me the permission. Jewel Kelley is a true American hero. I am so proud to be her daughter. And ladies, her courtship with Dr. Kelley was one of the exceptions I speak of. This man had to play by her rules; and even then, all the kids had to adjust. Our parents knew it was worth the time and effort.)

Needless to say, there had been a lot of typical divorced mama yelling and screaming in the household prior to the family merger. But after Dr. Kelley's arrival, things changed. Leon Kelley is a God-fearing man, the best example I have ever seen of a Christian who practices what he preaches. (He is a model parent and husband and probably the reason I am not married today. He set the bar real high.) Leon does not believe in spanking and as a father of young boys, he practiced what he preached. What I watched changed my understanding of discipline forever.

Leon and Billy

I first saw this with Leon's youngest child, my brother, Billy. Billy was one of the cutest and sweetest kids I'd ever seen. Because he was the youngest, he had to go to bed the earliest. And he hated it.

"Daddy, I don't want to go to bed," he'd whine.

"Come here boy," Leon would say. "Let me see your eyes."

Billy would widen his tired eyes as big as he could. And his daddy would take a look.

"Oh Billy, those eyes look tired to me. This is what I need you to do. Let's get you a bath. Then go lay yourself down in your bed for a few minutes. And one of the girls will come in to read to you. Let's see what happens. If you're not tired, you won't fall asleep. If you are and you go to sleep, I'll see you tomorrow, and you'll feel so good, you'll have a great day."

Of course, after a bath and a book, little Billy was fast asleep.

Observing this father-son relationship taught me so much. Billy was never an over active or "hyper" kid. My son, Winston, on the other hand, was energy overload (I wonder where he got it from). The lesson Dr. Kelley taught me was that when a kid does not want to go to bed, he's not being bad, he just doesn't want to miss out on the action. He also taught me that young kids need a lot of sleep. Putting a kid to bed is a process – a ritual of love. It involves a relaxing bath, a story, lights out and doors closed. It's hard for anyone to fight sleep under those conditions. But mostly it means not caving in. Bedtime is bedtime.

A kid can whine all he wants, but when the routine is established, that's it. There is nothing a kid can do about it. You just have to know that. And as a single mama, if you are not putting your kids to bed at a decent hour, you are going to be in a heap of trouble. You won't have time for yourself. And if your kid is like mine was, you'll have hell to pay the next day. Nothing tames a wild child like a good night sleep. (Pediatricians have a wide range of opinions about drugs that calm "hyper" kids. My favorite doctor, and you can just guess who that is, recommends you try the sleep routine, along with mealtimes and other rituals before considering anything stronger.)

Obviously discipline does not end with getting your kid to go to bed on time. But it is an outstanding beginning to getting you to put your foot down and enforce the law of your home – whether a mansion, house, condo, apartment or FEMA trailer. So much of discipline has to do with putting your kids' bodies and minds in a place where they can reason. That's why I started with emphasizing a good night's sleep and a time for bed, breakfast, homework, TV, dinner and a set bedtime.

I also believe strongly in taking things away from misbehaving kids, depriving them of their prized possessions, whether it's a favorite Teddy bear, pair of shoes or a CD player. When kids misbehave, call them on the carpet, floor or rug and make them own up. Then tell them to give you that thing they love so much. Let them know you'll be holding on to it for a set number of days (3-5) unless they give you cause to hold onto it longer. Tell them in no uncertain terms that if they do not act like they have some sense, you will sell the item and forget all about it.

Stick to your guns, Mama

Part of discipline comes with doing what you say -- being disciplined enough yourself not to change the punishment midstream. If your kids see that you are not serious about enforcing the law, they'll wear you down every time. Then see what happens when you try to take something away.

Discipline is not all about punishment. It's also about praise. I found that praise works best when it is delayed. In other words, if your son shares his candy bar with his sister in front of you, don't immediately say, "Oh, that's so sweet of you to share your candy." No. Instead hold off for a few minutes or hours. Then say something. Or be more creative than that. Send them a text message the next day or put a note under their pillow or in their lunchbox telling them what you saw. Let them know how you felt watching it and how you feel about them in general. That way, your kids won't only do the good stuff when the enforcer is watching. Remember, this is about creating systems for instilling *self*-discipline.

Long ago, when my son was still a baby, I attended a parenting class that was part of a group-counseling program. I learned a lot about the power of communication as a part of instilling self discipline. The biggest lesson is that parents should begin talking to their kids early; not badgering them and as my son says, interrogating them, but using skills that encourage them to open up and share with you.

Active listening 101

Here's an example from my own experience that I pass on to single mamas in my parenting classes. Ironically, it took place within weeks of my learning in the parenting class I took how to deal with this kind of thing.

Once, when Winston was about three years old and I picked him up from daycare, I asked him how his day went.

"Bad."

"Bad?"

"Yeah."

"Why?"

"Because no one would play with me."

"Sounds like that makes you feel pretty sad."

"Sad and mad."

"Well, what do you think you might do if that happens tomorrow?"

"I could beat everybody up."

"Yeah. But that would probably get you in trouble. What else could you do?"

"I could play with Emily. Nobody plays with her."

"Well, why don't you give it a try? And let me know how it goes."

"O.K."

This was a lesson in active listening; not running to your kids' rescue, but listening to how they feel so that they are safe enough to share it, no matter what. The purpose is to get your kids to be disciplined enough to work through their own problems – to consider the "what ifs" and to know that they can deal with life.

As children grow older, you want this to continue. You want them to feel as safe at 14 as they did as 4, whether the problem is not making the team or getting asked by their best friend to hit a joint. You cannot be there. They have to be self-disciplined and confident enough to make the right decisions, at least most of the time.

One of the best ways to instill self discipline is to be disciplined yourself, Mama. In other words, you must model the behavior you are trying to enforce. If you're asking your kids not to curse or wear inappropriate clothing or gossip, don't do these things yourself. I think with clothing and style, even when you're doing your best, your kids surprise you. And sometimes, according to Dr. Kelley, you have to let them dress a little crazy so that you can continue the open communication. Most of the time, hairstyles and fashion get ups are phases. But despite what your kids are doing, your best bet with getting them to at least set some limits is to set some limits yourself.

I'll never forget an incident that occurred when my son was in the 5th grade. I was living in St. Petersburg, Florida at the time. For whatever reasons, I was off one day during the week and able to pick Winston up from school. I was wearing some sort of short wraparound skirt, a midriff blouse and high-heeled sandals. I was a little early, so I got out of the car to meet my son.

When I picked him up, I saw a look on his face of disgust, but it was an expression I was not yet accustomed to seeing, not in his eyes, anyway. So I wasn't sure what was going on.

Once in the car, I asked, "How was today?"

"O.K."

"You don't sound O.K."

Silence.

"What's the matter? You look disgusted."

"Mom?" Winston asked. "Yes?"

"I'm not trying to be disrespectful, but could you do me a favor?"

"Uh...sure. What is it?"

"Next time you come to my school, will you *look* like a mother? I mean, what you're wearing -- it's embarrassing. And when you're a boy, it's hard enough trying not to get into a fight. But if somebody says something about your mother, you have to hit them."

I surveyed my outfit. I felt awful. I realized just how hoochie I looked. I was ashamed.

"Sure, Winston," I answered. "I'll do that. I'll look like a mother. And I'm sorry."

I was mortified. I couldn't wait to change. And to think...I really thought I was cute in that little ensemble. Sometimes, Mamas, you should ask a few people what they think of how you dress. If four of five say "kinda hoochie," believe them. And know that the fifth was probably being kind (or maybe she needs the hoochie check, herself). Don't step outside representing your family looking ridiculous.

Future school visits

I went to visit Winston at school throughout his school days, whenever I had an opportunity. I went when he got in trouble and just to show up. I went to talk to Winston's teachers and to remind him that I was on their side. (That helped me have a partner in getting him to behave.)

When we were in San Diego, I also raced from my job sometimes to show up during lunchtime to bring a surprise fast-food lunch to Vanessa, a girl at his school in my Sunday school class with whom I'd formed a big sister/mentor relationship. (Of course, I'd visit Winston and give him the same treat at these times, too. It was great because they were both at Roosevelt Junior High at the same time.) I believe showing up at your kids' schools announced or unannounced is important.

What I learned is any time Mama shows up; the kids are somewhat embarrassed (even when you're wearing a business suit). Whether they say so or not, they're also happy and somewhat proud that their mama cares. So I made a point to be there, even for a few minutes. But after that conversation in the car on the way from Bay Point

Middle School, every time I showed up, I was careful to make sure I looked like a mother.

Tips for Instilling Self Discipline

- **Enforce early bedtimes and establish comforting nighttime rituals to help your kids fall asleep**

- **Build a system of security by establishing routines for family meals, studying and playtime**

- **Be present to let them know they have your support, but let them lead the decision-making process**

- **Set a good example**

- **Don't come to your kids' rescue; instead work with them to find solutions to problems**

- **Give them delayed positive feedback (notes in their lunchbox, text messages, etc.) when they do something that makes you proud. On-the-spot praising might create a situation where your child only does good things if you or another adult is watching**

- **Show up at their school whenever possible**

- **Be on their teacher's side and make sure the kid and the teacher know it**

- **Get your children involved in Sunday school, sports and other structured activities (See chapter 6)**

- **Dress like a mother**

6

Do Get Your Kids Involved In Something Positive.

So what are your children doing when they're not at home or school? Are they good at anything in particular? Do they like to sing or act or play football or compete in spoken word competitions? What are their gifts and talents?

A good single mama must watch her kids and help them identify what makes them tick, what makes them proud and have self worth, self respect and self discipline.

One single mama who reached out to me through my website, singlemamahood.com, which has a Free Advice section, expressed her desperation with not one, but three children. (To protect the writer's privacy, I have changed names and some of the details of the email note.)

Her issues illustrate a single mama's need for an external support system of people and activities to reinforce her efforts at home. No single mama can do it alone.

Dear Ms. Kelly

I am not sure where to begin. I'm overwhelmed even thinking about my situation.

I am a single mama of three kids.

My oldest will be 12 next month and it seems as though I can't get him to listen. He stays in a playful mode all the time, even when I'm being serious with him. I should also mention that he has a serious attitude!

My second is 9. He pretends not to hear me. Most of the time, he refuses to cooperate, whether it's time for him to clean up or sit down and be still or eat. When I ask him to do something, he gets up and walks around, wastes time and just goes through the motions. He does not do as he is told. And he has some pretty bad anger issues.

My third child is five. She's my girl. She wants my full attention and will do what it takes to get it when she can. She's also pretty stubborn. She thinks she is supposed to have the last word with me and with everyone. I find myself arguing and trying to reason with a five-year-old.

Ms. Kelly, please help me find ways to get these kids to listen to me without yelling, screaming, fussing and cussing. So far, that's the only thing that gets their attention, for a little while, anyway. But it's making me sick.

I want my children to grow up to be respectful adults, but I'm afraid that will not happen unless I get some sort of control.

Please help.

Here was my response:

Dear Mama,

I suspect the children are craving structure. Structure has a way of making kids feel happy and secure (even if they do complain.)

I recommend you change the rules. But know that kids who are used to having chaos in their lives will simply not believe their mama is serious when she changes the rules. As for the anger and attitudes, next time one of your kids start talking mess, don't raise your voice, lower it. Tell them that if they raise their voices or do whatever else they are doing inappropriately, you will take away something away that they cherish. Then, follow through. Let them know that if they get violent with you, you'll have to get the police involved. Let them know how the system works and that they could end up in foster care, where they'd surely learn to appreciate you.

As part of the new household structure, tell them you all will start doing certain things at certain times. There will be a homework time, dinnertime, playtime, TV time and bedtime. Those who disobey will have privileges taken away. Also, as part of the structure, take them to church and Sunday school. You'll be surprised how much they'll like it, especially the younger ones.

Always tell them what to do in a low, monotone voice and do not let the kids interrupt you. That will get their attention. On the other hand, when the children do something right, take mental note. Then later, a few hours later or even the next day, pull them aside and tell them you are proud of them for what they did. You want to be careful not to praise them right away because you don't want them only doing the right thing when you or another adult is watching. You can also put notes in their lunch box or under their pillows, too.

Child number one – This kid probably needs something in his life that makes him feel good about himself. He also needs to know that being funny is cute, but that playing too much has consequences, like getting your favorite thing (a gadget, CD or favorite shirt) taken away for a few days. He needs to know that if inappropriate behavior continues, the thing will disappear. And you really do have to follow through, Mama. I would recommend some sort of competitive sport. What is he good at? Help him find an activity that has a male coach who can back you up on the discipline front. Church activities and the positive

messages he hears at church will help, too.
Second child -- He really needs to be
motivated. I recommend sports and church
activities for him too. Also, if he's strong at a
certain subject in school, give him the
responsibility of working with his younger sister on
homework.

Daughter -- She sounds like a bright kid who
can benefit from positive time with Mama. She
should have the benefit of a special routine every
night. She should get a bath and a book to make
bedtime special, especially because she loves her
mama's attention. As for her stubborn arguing,
just end the debates by telling her it's over. You're
the boss because you're the mother; let her know
that when she's the mother, she can be the boss –
but that she'll never be the boss of you.

Now, Mama, outside of work, you need to be
a full time mama. I'm not sure if this is an issue
for you, but you have no time to be trying to get a
man... Focus all of your attention on getting your
household in order and you'll attract positive
people in your life.

Take care and good luck. If these tips don't
work, I'll be surprised. Either way, see if you can
get some kind of professional counseling or
parenting support or help through your job or
community service center.

Oh, and always say positive things about
their dads; but be honest if you do not know why
they don't come around. They need to know that
any behavior from their father that they don't like
has nothing to do with them.

If they complain about being in a single
mama-headed household, tell them that you're

sorry they could not have had a more perfect family, but that you're doing your best and they can help by doing their best so that they can make good decisions and be good parents when they grow up and get married.

Ms. Kelly

A single mama needs a lot of support. All of her children should be involved in structured activities. Children need to understand that discipline is a part of society and that Mama is not the only person expecting them to live by rules and have order in their lives.

Kids need to feel special

Our children are like us. They want and need to feel important and they have to know they are special. Observe your children from when they are babies. As they grow, you'll notice that the core of their personalities remains the same. Kids who seem laid back, observant and quiet continue to be mellow. The ones who are bouncing off the walls don't stop. They keep bouncing throughout their childhood, pre-teen and teenaged years.

Little children will change their minds a lot about what they are interested in. Let their imaginations run wild. Do they like dinosaurs or dogs? Are they cat kids or are they more into reptiles? A fun activity, for me, anyway, is shopping at garage and rummage sales. Let your kids go with you and give them a couple of dollars. Show them how to negotiate and let them know that if they really like something to try to get the seller to lower the price.

During these outings, you'll see what your kids are drawn towards. For example, kids who like baseball will naturally be drawn to baseballs, gloves, bats and books about baseball and baseball players. The ones who like fashion will be drawn to the tables that display it. They'll play dress up and change outfits over and over. They'll probably have fashion shows for you and the family. Be there for them. Be their biggest fan.

When your kids change focus, that's OK. But if they have a particular mathematic, musical, artistic, sports or writing talent, encourage it and find a community resource that will allow them to explore and practice their skill so that their talent is enhanced.

A lot of parents push their kids towards the things they want their kids to do well. Try your best not to do this. Instead, know that single mamas' kids are easily drawn into circles of people who give them attention that you may not have time to give. Since you know you cannot always be there, find another trustworthy adult -- a teacher, coach or recreation coordinator -- who can help provide the balance your kids need. Again, all kids want to feel special. You have to pay very close attention to each of your kids to make sure they know that you value what makes each of them special and unique.

Part of identifying what makes your children tick is listening to them. If you're good about putting your kids on a schedule, establishing rituals and setting times for homework, mealtime, playtime, TV time, etc., you will have time to talk to them. I'm not talking about an hour a day per child. I'm only talking about 15 minutes or so of undivided time for each of them. During this time, there should be no TV or radio in the background. This is a time for you to give each of your children your undivided attention. Many kids cannot stand to give anyone more than a few minutes at a time, so don't force the whole 15 minutes if they don't give it to you.

During this time, you should ask your kids how school is going, how their social life is going, what they like about their lives and what they don't. When they tell you what they don't like, do not take it personally. They might say things that sound really small. They could also try to downplay things that bother or hurt them so as not to appear silly. On the other hand, more dramatic kids might make a big thing out of something that you think sounds small. Either way, your job during these periods is to listen.

More on listening actively

When you talk to your children, listen for words and observe body language that might illustrate how they feel about what they are experiencing. The key is to help them identify their feeling and assist them in finding a solution for the problem that's causing it. Then let them take the lead so that they feel empowered by solving their own problems.

For example, if your fifth-grade daughter tells you that the girls she used to play with now ignore her, listen to her tone. Does she sound angry or sad or left out? Then suggest what you think.

"Sounds like that makes you feel pretty sad," you might say. The child will usually answer back by either confirming what you believe or by rejecting it and offering what she is actually feeling, whether it is angry or lonely. Whatever the feeling, do not tell your child not to feel that way. You cannot control anyone's feelings. So don't try. Instead, ask your daughter what she might *do* if that kind of thing continues. You might offer a suggestion, such as, "Maybe you can start spending more time with people who appreciate you more, kids you feel good to be around." Or, "Your friend, Karen, would probably be happy to have you hang out with her again. You haven't spent time with her in a while."

Usually, those suggestions will trigger others from your child. If your daughter makes a suggestion that you know would have bad consequences, such as, "I could cuss all those girls in that little clique out," you should let her know that you understand how she feels but tell her that would probably result in negative consequences. When the conversation ends, make sure she feels that she has come up with a constructive solution. Then tell her to be sure to follow up and let you know how it goes.

I cannot say enough about active listening. In addition to being introduced to the communication technique shortly after my son's father and I separated, I've done a lot of reading about it over the years. I've practiced it so much that it's become almost second nature, but I still slip. Active listening makes me feel supportive and valuable in a relationship with children and adults. It's a way of really giving someone your attention.

With teenagers, who often have a hard time talking to anyone, especially their parents, it's a way of getting some real dialog going. The more you do it, the more natural you'll feel and the closer you will get to your kids. The toughest part is holding back.

You can't tell your kids how to feel or judge how they are feeling. You must hear them out, let them make suggestions, remind them of consequences if they suggest something harmful or ridiculous and allow them to think for themselves because ultimately, it's their problem and you cannot solve it. Yes, you can bandage it for a while by jumping to the rescue, but that will usually only cause your child to feel insecure and helpless. You want them to develop coping skills so that when problems occur down the line, they will not hesitate to make an attempt to solve them on their own.

The significance of meaningful activities

I cannot say enough about the importance of getting your children involved in meaningful activities. For me, the two keys were church activities and sports.

The Murphy's and others who came to this single mama's rescue

My best teacher for this is Louis Morris Murphy, Sr., now pastor of Mount Zion Progressive Missionary Baptist Church in St. Petersburg, Florida. Louis and his wife, Mina, their son, Louis ("LJ") and daughter, Chariga, were Winston's third family.

When they saw the close bond between our boys and realized that Winston was spending time after school at a neighborhood recreation center, they offered to babysit him (free of charge) -- to take him to football, basketball and track practices and let him spend time with them when I worked evenings and/or nights.

At the time, I was a TV news reporter, so there were many nights when I arrived to pick Winston up so late that he was already asleep. He spent more nights with the Murphy's than I can count. Single mamas rely so much on people like this beautiful family.

Before going on about the Murphy's, I should also mention that there were many extended family members in my life. Feron and Kim Gilmore and their five children were another family always willing to open their home and hearts for Winston and me. I met Kim while volunteering in a program to tutor adults who were studying for their high school equivalency exams. I do believe God puts people in our lives for a reason. We just have to be open to the blessing. I am so grateful that I was.

And I will never forget Mrs. Dorothy Sholes, my St. Petersburg neighbor who was there to meet Winston when he got off the school bus in kindergarten and first grade, just before we met the Murphy's. Mrs. Sholes was always there for us, and this meant the world to me.

Now back to Pastor Murphy. Louis (who was Mr. Murphy and later, Rev. Murphy then -- but always Louis to me and Uncle Louis to Winston) treated Winston just as he did his own son. Louis was adamant about the importance of getting kids involved in sports and church activities.

Mina, whom Louis met when he was in the military and stationed in Hawaii, grew up on the islands of Samoa. As a mom, she spent a lot of time teaching her children about her customs, history and traditions. So the kids would perform traditional dances whenever a neighborhood event or competition that offered the opportunity would present itself. Louis Sr. knew this was important to his wife and, therefore, made it a priority.

As for sports, Louis Murphy was the coach, the enforcer of discipline and practice. He saw to it that Winston, along with LJ, trained as though sports would be their livelihood some day. In fact, LJ is now a wide receiver on a football scholarship at the University of Florida. So the pastor's faith and hard work have already yielded quite a return. Louis Sr. saw to it that Winston competed with a passion, that he took sports seriously and learned lessons of character and competitiveness from his athletic activities.

In addition to encouraging Winston's pursuits on the athletic field (I should mention that my son was quite the little athlete, himself. A small but mighty kid, he played basketball and football throughout his youth and high school years), Louis saw to it that Winston studied the Bible. He held Bible study with his family just about every day. He also took Winston to church with his family when he was with them on weekends and quizzed Winston on the scripture.

Louis sat on the sidelines providing support for both his son and mine during football, basketball and track season. He took the kids to track meets and football games. He was often there for the boys during practices, too. And back home, he was there, along with Mina, to make sure the kids did their homework in the evenings.

Winston says Uncle Louis showed him the meaning of the love of Jesus. I know that Louis and his family were on a mission from the Lord when it came to my son. And they did a fabulous job. It really does take an entire community to help a single mama raise a child.

While we left St. Petersburg for California just before the boys entered middle school, LJ and Winston have remained friends. Through the magic of email and cell phones, their friendship survived our time in California, Winston's boarding school experience in Andover, Massachusetts and college in different cities. Louis Sr. revealed to me that the boys make regular road trips between Gainesville and Atlanta, where Winston attends Morehouse College.

Anyone who knows LJ will see an intensely compassionate, devoted, loyal young man. He and his family have been though a lot. One of their toughest challenges came several years ago when Mina was diagnosed with breast cancer. She went through treatment and I am so happy to say she is a survivor.

The Murphy's have remained strong and the family continues to be a role model unit and an inspiration to my son and me.

Here are some tips on making sure that your kids are involved in something positive.

- **Watch your children and talk to them often about their interests.**

- **Find some sort of athletic activity that you can get your children involved in and don't be afraid to ask for help from other families.**

- **Attend your children's sports activities and other events and when possible, even the practices. Take a front seat and make sure they know you are there. Praise them for participating and working hard.**

- **While relying on the help of family and friends is good, do not overstay the welcome or carelessly take advantage of the situation. (For example, I made sure that I kept LJ at my house as much as I could. At times, I even took Chariga on outings. And while they would not take money, I would insist that the Murphy's take an occasional bag of groceries or little treats that I'd drop off when I'd pick Winston up from their house.)**

- **Girls need sports as much as boys do. Studies find girls who are involved with** sports have higher levels of self-esteem and a lowered risk of getting involved in sexual activity.

• Find a church where you feel loved and needed and get your kids involved as soon as you can.

• If you did not grow up in church and feel intimidated about going, start by visiting your friends' churches. Trust me, when you are where you should be, you will get over it. Your kids need and deserve to know that they are a part of something much larger than home and school.

• Begin to explore your children's interests when they are very young. Exploring books about a variety of sports and talents is a good start.

7

Do Take Education Seriously.

I don't care whose statistics you're looking at, the bottom line is the same. Young people who complete a four-year college degree program have a better chance at being financially successful than those who don't. Sure, there's the exceptional entrepreneur, the super model or professional athlete or entertainer who made it without, but even they will often tell you that education gives you an advantage. That said, despite your kids' creative talents, please encourage them to study hard and do their best in school. Tell them to approach every day of their school days as though they are preparing to go to college.

So what if you didn't go to college? Often single mamas who barely got their high school education or GED feel intimidated by the idea of college. But ladies, just know that you aren't the first. Many successful people, particularly African Americans, in my age group (forty something) are in fact, first-generation college graduates. A lot of our parents didn't know either. But the good thing is they were not afraid to let us investigate, ask questions and go boldly forward, knowing that even if our mamas grew up on a farm picking cotton (and mine did), we were going to college. (In fact, by the time I got my degree, my mom had gotten hers too.)

So what do you do to support your child's dreams or encourage them if they have not yet formed thoughts about higher education? Well, start with not thinking you're too good to ask questions. I can't stand when people act all high and mighty to cover up some insecurity only to miss an opportunity that would have otherwise come their way. Their noses are so far up in the air that they miss the gifts right in front of their faces.

Here are some easily accessible resources for single mamas who don't know much about college, but for the sake of their kids, are willing to learn.

- **College Board (www.collegeboard.com)**

- **ACT, Inc. (www.act.org)**

- **The United Negro College Fund (www.uncf.org)**

- **Moms (or dads), single or married, who are college graduates. Find someone at work, church or in your social or parenting circles whom you trust, and don't be allow fear or embarrassment to get in the way of your asking them about what you don't know.**

- **College counselors at your kids' schools**

- **Your pastor – pastors are great resources for college information because lots of colleges utilize them as a way to recruit students**

- **People in your family who graduated college. Again, this is not the time for pride. We're talking about your**

children's education, and nothing should get in the way.

It is also important to let your kids explore options on their own. If you are unfamiliar with what they're talking about – all the chatter about PSATs, SATs, ACTs and the like, please ask. There are things you should know about these tests, such as deadlines, number of times your kids can take the tests, fees, registration, etc.

As you start getting into the "My kid's going to college" frame of mind, please already be prepared for the fact that your child is growing up. I say this because way too often, I hear stories of single mamas who don't want to let go. What that's all about, I cannot relate, but what I can tell you is that a grown child who is living in your house, not paying rent, unable to keep a job, is not the goal we're after. We are talking about rearing self-sufficient, independent young men and women who get their education, see the world, get married, have children of their own, and visit – that's VISIT their mama regularly. Let go of your kids; you're not doing them any favors by holding on. (Please note that exceptions here are children who, as a matter of cultural tradition and custom, return to the family home, pooling their financial resources with their siblings and parents, after college and even after marrying.)

The other day, I was in the grocery store and heard a conversation behind me that I could not help butting into. A 19-year-oldish African

American guy had run into a childhood friend, an attractive young lady.

"I thought you had gone away. Someone said you went to Ireland to go to college. Didn't you have a scholarship?"

"Yeah; but I ended up staying. And, you're right; I had a scholarship and everything. But my mom didn't want me to go. She's sick now and on dialysis."

"Well, that's nice of you to stay and take care of her," the young woman said.

"Actually, she's doing OK and my sister is looking after her. I really think she just wanted me to be closer to her."

"My mother would have told me to go on and take the opportunity," the woman said. "Knowing her – and she's a single mom and I'm her only child," she wouldn't have wanted me to miss that opportunity. Shoot, that's an opportunity of a lifetime!"

I don't think the young man knew what to say. So I said something.

"Maybe you can explain to the college that your mom got sick and ask them to hold the scholarship for you until next year."

"I thought of that," he said. "But I just think my mom wants me to stay in Chicago. I think she would have wanted me to stay close to her even if she wouldn't have gotten sick. She never wanted me to even leave Chicago for school, let alone go to another country."

I smiled and turned around and decided to check out my items and mind my own business. I could not help but think this child's mom was not unlike many single mamas. This is one thing about a lot of single moms, even married ones, that I just don't get. How can we not want our kids to experience life in a bigger way than we did? How can we want to keep them up under us, as we say, for some ridiculously long period of time? Don't you know, Mama, that kids are supposed to grow up? Don't you know that young people who are forced to be independent make more productive, contributing adults?

Let's let our kids grow up. They have to. We are not doing them any favors by babying them. I see women still cooking, cleaning and washing clothes for grown folks just because they gave birth to them. Being a good mama means grooming kids to become independent adults.

Start at the Beginning

If your child is still a baby, you are lucky to be getting this information now. The earlier you start supporting your kid's educational pursuits, the better. In fact, there are even studies now that show that babies whose mothers read to them before they are born are at an advantage. I'm not sure about all that, but I do believe the sooner you start disciplining yourself to do what it takes to give your child a love for knowledge, the better. You and your children will learn a lot in the process.

When your baby is still an infant, buy as many baby books as possible. They are often on sale at bookstores and even Sam's Club. When people ask you what you need for the baby, please do not forget to tell them books.

An extra step

For mamas of children of color, I highly recommend books with pictures of people who look like them. In fact, I believe all children should see diverse cultural images in the books they read, beginning with their first picture books. You don't have to do this to the exclusion of buying books with pictures of white kids. It's just that raising African American and other children of color with high self-esteem takes some extra steps. Minority children are bombarded with negative images of kids and adults who look like them. As their primary parent, you have to counter that as much as possible. I believe all kids benefit from associating learning with images of kids from all walks of life (including children who have disabilities). I absolutely love seeing little African-American girls pampering their black dolls.

Sadly, studies report many African American kids, even in the 21st century, prefer white dolls because they believe white children are better than they are. (This is a whole other topic; I mention it, however, because children of single mamas are really in trouble if they have race-related inferiority complexes.) I really think it's cool when white girls have dolls of different colors. It says a lot to me about their mamas.

Buying books is something that I want all single mamas to get in the habit of doing. It's something that should happen throughout your kids' lives so that they have their own library.

When your kids are babies, begin reading to them every night. This is an important part of their bedtime ritual. As you read to them, point to the words. As toddlers, your youngsters will begin to understand that you are sounding out words. Now, I'm no teacher, but I have practiced this routine with several children, including my little brother and my son. Before they were in kindergarten, they were sounding out words.

Please tell anyone who watches your babies during the day when you are at work to take time to read to your children. If the babies have favorite books, it's OK to read those books over and over. The purpose of reading to your babies is not to try to create prodigies (although that's fine, too); it's to give them a love for reading, learning and discovery. So if you've never bought your kid a book, make that your next purchase. And if you cannot afford to buy one, get a library card.

When School Starts

By the time your kids start school, they will have a head start. They will understand what school is all about and be ready to learn. They will associate learning with kids of all races because they will be used to seeing all those wonderful pictures in their books. You must make sure your kids have high self esteem and are proud of the fact that they are smart. Any time you get an indication that they are trying to hide their intelligence, please tell them that most kids want to be successful. This is something I truly believe. Let them know that many children are afraid of taking a chance at working to become smarter because they believe they are going to fail. So these negatively behaving children just keep on doing what they are good at, whether that's teasing other kids, making jokes or just being a bully. While your kids do not have to rub their intelligence in the faces of their peers, they should be proud of whom they are. And when they can, they should offer to help their peers who are willing to learn.

Get your kids jazzed about school

Talk about school in positive terms. "You're so lucky, you get to got to school!" Make sure they know that you are going to make sure they go to bed early so that they can be rested and have a good day at school. Tell them that's why you want to get them up early in the morning, too. Let them know that they will think more clearly and be more ready to learn when they have good night's sleep. Here, you are getting them in the habit of being self-disciplined because as they get older, they'll need more than Mama's nagging to study.

When your baby's in first grade, you should begin the ritual of homework. This should continue until your kids are out of the house and off to college.

Here are some tips for helping your kids with their homework:

- **Establish and enforce a "one-hour homework time" rule. The best time is as soon as your kids get home from school, after-school day care or sports activities. Homework time means no TV, phones or text messaging. If your kids claim they have no homework, insist that they read until the hour is up. (If their workload requires more than one hour, by all means, let them take more time!)**

- **Homework hour should include a healthy snack, such as fresh fruit.**

- **Be with your kids when they are doing homework. This will encourage them to talk about subjects they find interesting or difficult. If homework time is while you're at work, insist that your kids take note of what they liked and did not enjoy about their homework so that they can share it with you when you get home.**

- **If your children are struggling with an assignment, ask questions to assist them with figuring out the answers. In cases where you find the material difficult to grasp, admit it. Write a note to your child's teacher requesting a meeting in person or on the phone to come up with a solution for getting your child extra help or tutoring.**

- **Just as you establish homework hour, schedule play time, dinnertime, TV time and bedtime. These routines will help instill self-discipline. Share meals with your kids.**

- **Bedtime should be early on weekdays, 8 p.m. – 9 p.m. for primary school students, 9 p.m. – 10 p.m. for middle school kids, and not much after 10:30 p.m. for high school students. Bedtime means no phone, text messaging or computers, but it can and should include reading. With younger children, bedtime should follow bath time and** include a bedtime story from Mama. If you work nights, give this assignment to a trusted babysitter or older child. This is an important ritual that encourages a lifetime love for reading and learning.

- Use school as a topic for regular discussion with your kids. Without interrogating them, ask them what they think of certain subjects they are studying. This will make school more interesting to them and alert you to all kinds of issues your kids might not ordinarily feel comfortable talking to you about.

- Drop by your child's school. Let teachers see your face, even if only for a few minutes, and let the teachers know you are on their side. This will keep your kids from playing you and their teachers against one other.

- Stay engaged. Being a good parent takes time, energy, dedication and hard work.

- Take time to relax and unwind. This is why established, enforced bed times are good for you, too. Once your kids are in bed, you'll have at least an hour or so for yourself. The more rested you are, the easier it will be to support your child with school and homework and anything that might be getting in the way of their success.

8

Do Stay Close To Your Teenagers.

One of the toughest periods of single mama's life is a time that starts when your kids are about 12 years old. This is the time your children will test their limits and yours. They will want to experiment with different styles, friends and approaches to life. They will feel insecure, afraid and out of control. Often, they won't know what they are experiencing, which will make all the conflicting feelings even more difficult for them to deal with. Hey, we were all teenagers, and we know what we went through. Our kids are no different. They'll just have more resources and opportunities to test their limits. That's what makes raising teenagers so frightening.

My advice is to know that no matter what your kids say and despite their body language, they'll need if not want you to continue to provide some guidance and structure in their lives. When I ask teenagers what they want from their parents, they often say time. When I share this with moms, there is often confusion. They think that's the last thing their teenager would want from them.

Transition time

When my son was a teenager, he was moody. He's a kid who is extremely bright, creative, gregarious, outgoing and success oriented. So his teenaged years were a time when he felt under a lot of pressure, when he knew every decision mattered and almost everything counted. Teenagers hear that nearly every day. It's bound to make them worry about whether they will be ready for the next stage.

Fortunately, Winston's a talker, so he never held back in describing to me exactly what he was going through. He worried about everything from whether he was liked by his peers to whether he was going to get into the colleges he applied to. Sometimes the fear of what was to come was paralyzing. He'd procrastinate and procrastinate about applications and studying, until the very last minute. Everything seemed so overwhelming, what he was going to wear to prom, what his date was wearing, whether he'd stay in touch with his friends, whether some friends were really his friends. If you have teenagers, you know what I'm talking about. If not, try to remember what you went through as a teenager, and get ready.

Denise and Nedra

A friend of mine, Denise, is experiencing being the mama of a teenager right now with her daughter, Nedra. When she asks her daughter how things are going with certain programs or classes, Nedra completely freaks out.

"Mom, please, she moans, "this is already stressful enough."

Denise has asked me for advice. I suggested that her job is to find a way to be supportive without being pushy. She told me she has tried a number of approaches, but nothing seems to work. So I offered that she might try what worked most of the time for me and what seems to work for so many single mamas -- our tried and true method of active listening.

I told Denise that she might want to detach herself from the situation. This is a lesson I learned from Winston. He often told me that I couldn't worry about him as though his life were mine. I shared this with Denise and suggested that in the case of her daughter, she might remind herself that she is supporting her daughter, not living Nedra's life for her. I suggested that she check in with Nedra about how things are progressing. She should let her talk and ask questions. Instead of interrogating the girl, she should listen for words that describe how she is feeling – words such as "stressed," and "happy" and "sad" and "frustrating" and "scared."

Before Denise embarked on this new method of communicating with her daughter, we role-played. I played the role of Nedra. After I expressed words or body language that seemed associated with certain "feeling" words, I'd encourage Denise to simply say, "that sounds scary," or "you must be excited" or "confused." Denise saw how that created a safe environment for me to express myself. And it opened an opportunity for both of us to suggest solutions and for me to settle on one that made sense for me.

Once Denise felt confident, she tried it at home. She told me it felt awkward at first, but is working remarkably well. With her mama's support, Nedra is coming up with solutions that allow her to see through all the clutter.

For example, she told me Nedra finally knows what to do about her college applications.

"I decided I'm going to do one early application. Then I'll do only a few more, but only for schools I really want to go to. At least one of those schools should accept me," she told her mama.

Denise told me that Nedra regularly changes her mind about a decision, but being able to come up with a solution and voice it makes her feel more control of her own situation. After all, she is the one coming up with the answers.

It is important to remember that although teenagers may act aloof and uninterested in their parents, for the most part, they still crave our approval. Since we, as single mamas are the parent with which they are in most contact, our opinion matters.

Mamas tell me they believe their kids seem to care more about their fathers' approval. I felt that way, myself. But Dr. Kelley told me that's common. He said kids, like adults, naturally are more insecure about the opinion of the parent with whom they spend less time. When you are the primary custodial parent, your opinions and views matter; but your children may feel that your love is more unconditional because you are always there through the good, bad and ugly.

When kids are teenagers, they are at one of the most insecure points in their lives. We must remember that when they share with us, they are hoping we will approve of their honesty, initiative and choices. It's easy to jump in when our kids open up to tell us what we don't like and natural to want to share our own opinions. I'd advise you to listen carefully, take a deep breath, compliment them about what they did right in terms of taking time to think about their future, then help them as they come up with some options that you believe might have better consequences than ideas they may have come up with on their own.

Motivating teenagers

Not long ago, I did a parenting session at a Chicago high school. The topic was "Motivating Teenagers." The purpose was to give parents tools to communicate with their teens to find out just how motivated they are to set their beyond-high school futures into motion, and to show the teens that mama has their back. (No dads were at this particular session, although they were welcomed and I do hope some are reading now.)

One of the participants was a teenager, a high school senior, who attended with her mom. Her mom was not there for her daughter, but for her son, who was a junior.

We began the session with a visualization exercise. I asked everyone to close their eyes and to imagine that their children had graduated high school and were living their early adult years successfully. I asked them to think of all the details of what this looked like to them. After a while, I asked them to open their eyes.

Then the parents shared what they visualized.

One mom said, "I saw my son as a police officer. He was surrounded by his family. Everyone was really happy. He was very successful."

Another said, "My daughter was an attorney in court. She was dressed in a really nice business suit and she was arguing in court."

A grandmother said, "My granddaughter was a fashion designer." She was at a fashion show and all the models were wearing her designs."

I asked the parents to close their eyes again. This time, I asked them to describe what they felt as they visualized their children's success stories. They thought about it for a while, and then opened their eyes. The feelings they shared were pride, relief, joy, and happiness.

Then I asked the parents how attainable they thought these stories were. How confident, I asked, were they that these things would happen for their kids. The parents were hesitant to say they believed things would work out as they visualized it. They expressed doubt. Then we talked about why.

As is the case with many parents of teenagers, this group felt they could not connect with their kids in order to even find out what was going on with them from day-to-day, let alone where they were in terms of planning for their future. We talked about things that matter to their children, their "touch points." The parents mentioned music, cell phones, sports, friends, sweethearts, piercings, tattoos, and movies – all the things that matter to their teens. Then I asked my trick question.

"When I ask teenagers what they want from the parents, what do you guess the number one answer is."

The parents didn't answer. So I asked the high school senior who was there with her mom.

"What's the answer?" I asked.

"Time," she said.

"Absolutely right," I responded.

The parents were surprised. They couldn't believe it.

"Yes," I said. "That's what kids tell me. They want to spend time with you."

The problem is that most parents don't know this. When their kids are teenagers, everything would suggest just the opposite. Kids are coming and going, sharing very little with their parents. So the message appears to be that they don't want to be bothered. In fact, teenagers would love to spend more time with their parents.

Given that little known "touch point," I asked the parents to select one of the things that matters to their kids that also matters to them. The small group agreed that the thing they all shared in common with their kids was a love of going to the movies.

So I gave them a homework assignment. I suggested that they make a date with their teenager, to have the kids select a movie and set a time when they would take them on a date. If they had two teenagers, they would have to do two separate dates. Then I gave them a lesson in how to use the date as an opportunity to find out what's in their kid's head and how they could support their dreams of success.

The most important thing about the exercise is that the parent has to use the date opportunity to listen, learn and provide support, not to lecture. The point of the exercise is that the kid has to be the one to set, own and take steps towards accomplishing his goals. As a parent, your role is to remind the kid that these things have to happen and to ensure them that they have your support.

During the workshop, we conducted a role-playing exercise. Each parent pretended to be the child of the parent with whom they partnered. The actual conversation would take place after they saw the movie, at dinner, usually at a fast food restaurant of the kid's choice.

"So I remember you said you wanted to be a police officer. I know you have a lot going on right now, but is that something you're still thinking about?"

"Yeah, but you're right; there is a lot going on. So much is going on, I haven't had time to really do anything to plan my future."

At this point, I encouraged the person in the parent role to comment on what they believe the kid might be feeling.

For example: "It sounds like you're feeling overwhelmed."

Feeling validated, the child is then likely to talk a bit more about his feelings.

"Yeah, it is overwhelming... and kind of scary."

At this point, I encouraged the parents to ask the child what he or she has done to set the wheels of their future into motion. If the kid can't think of anything, the parent can make suggestions.

"Well, you picked up that application a month ago."

Then the kid will likely think of some things that he's doing on his own. At this point, I suggested that the parents should praise their teens for what they are doing. After that, the parents should ask what they could do to support their kids.

The high school senior who attended the workshop, who at the time was playing the role of her brother, made simple suggestions -- things like, "you can wake me up earlier" or "you can remind me to do my homework."

I told the parents that their kids' suggestions are likely to be very simple things. Still, I told them they should tell the kids to give them a code word to use should they need a reminder of where the nagging is coming from. It will be coming from their agreement, the contract between the parent and the teenager. And the best thing of all from the conversation is that the child will feel empowered to focus on his future, knowing that his parent is there for them.

We did more role-playing. The parents were amazed. They could not believe that something so simple could produce such important results.

At the end of the workshop, I asked the parents to close their eyes again. I told them to, again, imagine that their kids are a success. I told them to think about what that looks like – what it feels like. After a few moments, I told them to open their eyes.

Again they told me it felt great.

"How attainable does it seem now?" I asked. They all agreed that it felt very attainable, very realistic. And what's more, they knew they didn't have to do any real work. The work was up to their teenagers. All they had to do was come up with the best way to help empower their teens by casting a net of support.

*Here are some tips for breaking
the ice with your teenagers:*

- **Know that your kids still need you**
- **Make an appointment to spend some one-on-one time with your teenagers and let them pick the activity. Use that as an opportunity to find out what's on their mind**
- **Tell your teenager you know he/she has a lot going on. Ask how you can help sort things out and make things easier**
- **Check in with your teen regularly. Make periodic appointments away from home specifically to talk about things like college exams, applications, jobs, etc.**
- **Set new rules whenever new responsibilities or privileges become a part of your teens' lives. Make the rules a contract, if necessary, where you both sign off**
- **Enlist support from your teenager's favorite non-parent adult, -- teacher, coach, Sunday School teacher, relative or friend -- someone whom both of you trust**
- **Demonstrate approval when your teenagers show you that they are responsible. Even at this age, they really do still want to please you.**

One of the things teenagers say they are most afraid of is that their parents won't approve of them. They say this is why they do not open up more when they are around their single mama. Remember, as their primary parent, you matter more than you know.

9

Do Make Sure Your Kids' Values Are Straight.

Whenever I mention in a small crowd that I'm writing this book for single moms, someone tells me to be sure I speak to the importance of values. Usually these are people who have no children but have a lot of influence on our community's economic success. They are business owners and corporate executives. They are people who comment pretty regularly on how they believe our kids' values are too tied up in music videos, bling and sex.

Fortunately, having the perspective of being a parent makes me more optimistic about the outlook of our young people. I get to see all sides. So while I see a lot of the bling worship, I get to see some young people who are incredibly caring, giving, intelligent and compassionate. But I cannot argue with the fact that parents probably need tools to assist them in ensuring that their kids develop a healthy value system.

So while it's true that we should begin instilling good values in our children when they are babies, we have to start where we are. Wherever your kids are, it is not too late to begin to talk to them about kindness and goodness. If you are the parent with whom your child spends most of his or her time, you have more influence on them than you know. It's up to you to come up with ways to open your kid's eyes to ways in which they can make a contribution to their community and society as a whole.

Where do you start?

Several years ago, I had the opportunity to meet a young man who taught me a lot about how kids develop negative values. It's always been amazing to me that you can see two beautiful babies born the same day and one goes in a positive direction and the other ends up doing horrible things that hurt people.

When I met Jerome, I understood that kids are in fact innocent until something happens that turns their world into a nightmare. It's hard to wake up morning after morning from a bad dream and not accept that as your reality, but rather to get over it and move on. Fortunately, there are exceptions. And kids rise up from the ashes of horrible childhood circumstances to do great things. But many kids, perhaps most who are victims of ugliness when they are young end up repeating what they know.

I met Jerome when I was a reporter in the Tampa Bay area. I was asked by the local chapter of a non-profit organization to kick off a walk in the city of St. Petersburg. During the walk, I noticed that there were only three black people in the crowd – myself and two young men wearing hoodies with the hoods covering their heads. After everyone got moving, I joined the two young guys.

The curious reporter kind of gal that I am, I immediately struck up a conversation. By the end of the walk, I'd learned a lot about the boys. One was 16. His name was Mack. The other was Jerome. He was 17. They were both in juvenile detention, living in a halfway house across the street from the church that pulled strings to allow them to go on the outing. They had been attending the church. In fact, it was the only thing they were allowed to do outside of the walls of the halfway house.

Jerome and Mack told me that they were both foster kids. I can't remember what Mack's crimes were, but Jerome had been a car thief. He told me that he was four years old when he was removed from his home. His sister was a baby. They both ended up in separate homes.

Throughout Jerome's younger years, he took pride in the fact that he was a good student. He was an obedient child who cleaned up his foster parents' homes (he'd been in several) and he always wanted to make people happy. Still, he told me that when he fell short, he endured awful beatings. And he could not recall one time when a foster parent bought him new clothes.

When Jerome was about 11 years old, other kids began to tease him. They talked about his matted hair (his foster parents rarely took him for a haircut or told him how to take care of his hair). They also laughed at his tattered clothing and made him feel badly about not having real parents.

Jerome told me this is about the time he started hustling. He had to figure out how to get money to get haircuts, new clothes and cool sneakers. Some drug dealers hired him to be a lookout. It was easy. Before he knew it, Jerome was buying bootleg jeans, jerseys and sneakers. And the big boys he was hanging with hooked up his head.

Soon, Jerome graduated to stealing cars. That's when he got busted for the first time. In fact, every time he got in trouble, it was tied to stealing cars.

For whatever reasons, I liked this kid, Jerome. He was smart and honest, a leader. He was also a crack baby. So he was kind of funny looking in a cute sort of way. He had a great sense of humor and a quick mind.

At the end of the walk, when I told the boys I was going to write to them and visit them at the halfway house, I was serious. But they didn't believe me.

Getting to visit them was extremely difficult. I called the people who ran the house and they told me that only family members were allowed to visit, and only on Sundays. "But these two kids are foster children," I replied. "They don't have any family to visit them." The man responded by telling me how foolish I was for believing what these two criminals told me.

But I was a TV news reporter. So I knew how to get into places where people told me I could not go. I pulled strings and made arrangements to visit the boys on Sundays. I told Winston all about it. He was about 8 at the time. He looked forward to meeting the kids.

On our first Sunday, we did what most of the other families did. We brought fried chicken, potato salad, chips, fruit and sodas for a picnic. Then we showed up. They could not believe it. I know for sure that Jerome wanted to cry, but he was trying to be hard. He had to.

The halfway house allowed the families to meet with their kids in the parking lot. So that's what we did. We played music that Mack and Jerome liked. Jerome's hero was Tupac. Hanging out with those kids was so cool. They told us a lot about their childhoods. It was sad. The boys liked Winston a lot and he liked them. While I was not willing to put in the real work it would take to try to save the boys, I was glad that even for the five or six months of Sundays that we went to visit with them, we gave them something to look forward to. And they did the same for us.

The juvenile detention people assured me that when Jerome turned 18 that next April, he would be sent to a transitional living facility. On his birthday, I sent him balloons and cookies. He was so thankful and extremely happy. No one had ever done anything like that for him. He wrote me a very nice letter. I never said what a good writer Jerome was. But I'll tell you now. That kid was gifted and talented.

About a week later, Jerome called me in the middle of the night, collect. He was two counties away in an adult homeless shelter. That's where they dropped him off when he got out of the home. They told him good luck and have a nice life.

Needless to say, I let Jerome stay with us for a while. On his first day there, I came home late at night to the smell of bleach. Jerome had cleaned my house better than I ever had.

"Why'd you do that?" I asked. "I always clean up when I get new foster parents," he told me. I assured him I was no foster mama. No one was paying me to keep him. I made no promises I couldn't keep. I told him I was going to help him find a job or get into school and locate a transitional living situation for him.

Throughout the time Jerome was at our house, I could not get over how smart he was. Nor could I get over his low self-esteem. One time, we were filling out an application together for a transitional home for him. The application asked him to list five positive things about himself. Jerome just stared at the paper.

"What's the matter?" I asked him. "It's this question," he replied. I read the question.

"Jerome, that should be easy," I said. "Just think about it for a few minutes. You'll think of something. Just start with the fact that you're a good writer." He wrote that down and I went into the kitchen to cook dinner."

When I returned to the dining room, Jerome was at the table with his head down. The application was torn into shreds. Fortunately, I had another copy of it. After dinner, we worked through it together.

Jerome made it into the transitional apartments. He did well for a couple of months. But eventually, he got into trouble. He and his roommate stole a stereo from someone's car. They ended up in jail. Eventually, the two of them left the state and went to West Virginia. We stayed in touch for a while so I knew when he got busted for selling drugs and ended up in prison. Eventually, we lost contact altogether.

One day, years later, Winston and I were moving. We found a file that held all the letters Jerome had written me. Winston was amazed. "Mom," he said. "Look at these letters! I didn't know Jerome wrote this well."

I told Winston that I always knew Jerome was smart. The problem is, he didn't know. I told Winston that I think the biggest difference between him and Jerome was that Winston had parents and Jerome was on his own -- no mama or daddy to serve as the kind of security blanket a smart, creative, risk-taking kid needs. Jerome never had the assurance of knowing that no matter what, his parents loved him. Without that, he could not beat the demons that pulled him in the wrong direction. Some kids can do that. Unfortunately, Jerome just couldn't.

Your kids have you

I shared this story with you because your kids have you. So they have a chance to know good from evil and to choose good. But you have to be constantly in their faces to remind them of what's good and what's evil. You have to tell them that just as they feel good when someone smiles at them or says something nice to them, they can make someone's day with a small act of kindness.

Ask a little kid how his day was, and he'll describe it in simple terms, happy, sad, good, bad, that kind of thing.

When you ask why, the answer is also simple. "Because Rodney played with me." Or "because my teacher was nice to me" or "because nobody talked to me."

When kids get older, they lose touch with the simplicity of what makes or breaks a bad day. It's especially complicated with many boys. By about age five, they learn that expressing disappointment with what people don't give in terms of a smile or friendship is looked upon as "soft." So despite the fact that they still want people to treat them nicely, boys often do not express kindness with others.

But Mama, it's your job to remind kids that they should treat people the way they expect to be treated. This is one of the most important things about establishing good values. Teaching kids the importance of being nice to other people is a way of letting them know that you value that kind of treatment. And it's an easy lesson to learn and embrace.

Mama, because you are the primary parent, you have to constantly work on the values thing. But you need reinforcements. If you are not a person who feels comfortable with church, I strongly suggest that you do some shopping around. It is important that you find a house of worship where you feel your kids are being taught and shown good values. When I say shop, I mean it. Do not feel forced to be in a place that doesn't feel right. Also know that any church you join is only as good as the members. So when you feel comfortable with a church, get involved. Find out how you can put your talent to use and do it. This is the best way to be a good example for your children.

Make sure that you constantly tell your kids that while it is good for them to work towards earning a good living, they should not become consumed with making quick money. Let them know that it really is more important to give than to receive. Let them see you helping your neighbor and striving to be a good, decent human being. I've said this before and I'll say it again, kids do as they see, not just as they are told.

Surround them with good examples because with what they see on TV and in the streets and at school, they will need all the reinforcements you can give them.

Tips for strengthening your kids' values

- Watch TV with your children and explain right from wrong and good from bad

- Select books and movies to share with your kids that have story lines that deal with kindness, generosity and love

- Reward your children's kind deeds with positive notes and special times with you, such as a special early morning breakfast or a dessert date

- Expose your children to people who earned their wealth the hard way; if you do not know any of these people, read about them and share the stories with your children

10

Do Not Make Your Love Life More Important Than Your Parenting Responsibilities.

Busted.   Caught you reading the last chapter first! I thought I'd save the best for last.

On my singlemamahood.com website, the dating section of the Forum is its most visited area. Everyone wants love, and there's nothing wrong with that. I do, however, caution single mamas to remember that they are more mama than single. That means they have to follow a different set of rules than do single women with no children. Clearly, single mamas know this. Still, we do not always follow our own rules. Do we, Mama?

I would suggest, as I do when asked about dating during my speaking engagements, that single mamas always keep their kids' perspective in mind when they are dating. What would my kids think of how I'm pursuing this guy? What would my kids think if they or their friends saw me with this guy? What would my kids think if I married this guy?

Yeah, yeah, I know you're the adult and you owe your kids no explanation, but come on Mama, someone in the family has to have a conscience. Plus, what would you do if you got pregnant and this guy was the father? You'd have a lot of explaining to do.

There are some basic dating rules that most single mamas I speak to say they are aware of and follow most of the time. I state them here, because if you ask kids of single mamas, they'll tell you that many of their moms do not follow the rules. And the examples their moms are setting send their kids all the wrong messages, about how they feel about themselves and their kids.

Here are some tips on keeping your love life in perspective:

- **Read chapter 2.**

- **Maintain your role as the disciplinarian; let your honey observe your approach** and learn from it so that he knows the deal and both of you can make an early decision about whether he's up to the challenge.

- Once you believe a guy is serious (and you know he's not a pedophile), slowly let him get to know your children and spend time together without your being there with them.

- Listen to your children's feelings about your guy and understand that it is natural for them to feel threatened by his presence.

- Talk to your guy about the fact that your family life is a good one and that it will take time for your children to get used to the fact that things might be changing.

- Take extra steps to continue to spend time alone with each of your children.

- If you accept a marriage proposal and your children seem to be acting out because of it, seek pre-marital counseling for the entire family.

- Do not put the guy's needs before your children's needs. In other words, if you're the one buying, shopping and cooking, please do not save the biggest

steak, pork chop or piece of chicken for him. Your kids will think you are needy and pathetic. And the guy will know it's OK to disregard your hard work, responsibilities and your children.

- **Do not act like a wife until you actually are one.**

Ms Kelly takes the hard line

I communicate on my website with a single mama who struggles a lot with my dating rules. She thinks I am inflexible and just don't understand that some women's loneliness is such that they cannot easily follow my dating rules. To that I say, this guy is not your husband.

I've also run into single mamas who use the Bible to justify how they spend so much time serving their boyfriends' needs, even at the expense of their kids. But ladies, please do not be confused. The following refers to husbands, *not* boyfriends.

22Wives, submit to your husbands as to the Lord. 23For the husband is the head of the wife as Christ is the head of the church, his body, of which he is the Savior. 24Now as the church submits to Christ, so also wives should submit to their husbands in everything. (Ephesians 5:22-24)

If you are a single mother, you head your household; your boyfriend does not. He has not earned that right, as husbands do. And even in marriage, love and honor go both ways.

Do not believe the hype. There are worse things than being a single mama.

This is my final chapter, so I am trying to end on a high note. However, I just received an email from someone through singlemamahood.com who told me how she spent her day at the police station with a young single mother who is a victim of domestic violence at the hands of her boyfriend. Old ladies have told me so many times that you can "do bad all by yourself." Please know this, Mama. There is so much hype in our society about "having a man" that we often settle, especially those of us who are single mamas and desperate or anxious to fix it.

Deanna

I have a friend in Jacksonville, Florida, whom I'll call Deanna. Deanna and I used to watch each others' kids so that we could have some time to ourselves. She ended up meeting a guy named Hoarce and after a few months, married him. Hoarce was divorced and had two kids of his own. So for starters, although he was able to contribute to Deanna's income, he often had to tap into her meager funds as well.

Often after marrying Hoarce, Deanna found herself more broke than she was when she was alone. After a couple of years of fighting with Hoarce and her kids, who yearned for the days when he was not around, Deanna realized that she married Hoarce so that she could wear a ring and call herself Mrs. instead of a single mama. She thought he'd bring security and wholeness to her family.

Instead, he brought another set of issues with which she had to deal – more kids, less money, less time to spend with her own kids and mounting debt because Hoarce liked to invest and experiment with new business ideas. And after all, he was her husband, and Deanna is a Christian, so she worked hard to submit. But after a couple of years, she concluded it was too big a responsibility and they went their separate ways.

Take your time, Girl

What single mamas have to be honest about is that a good man is really hard to find. A lot of the guys who you are spending your precious dollars on to look and smell good for are really not worth it. Call me a male basher if you'd like; but I even had a guy tell me that he takes as much as he can from women because "they're willing to give and expect nothing in return."

"Women show us how to treat them," he said. "If they put us before their kids and we don't want to marry them anyway, hey it's not our problem."

Thankfully, not all guys are like this.

Put your family first and you'll be fine

The point is that if you put your family first and truly work to be the best mama you can be, you will be your most beautiful. Perhaps then you will not be the kind of woman a guy thinks he can take advantage of. Men will get to know you on your "I'm working on being a good mama" terms, and unless they are just cold hard, they'll respect you. Who knows, you might even attract the kind of man who honors you and your family and will add to what you have, not take away from it.

Singlemamahood should be about honoring yourself in ways that you never have. It's a time to realize that you have before you the greatest opportunity a woman can have, the chance to influence and shape the life of the greatest gift available to womankind – a child.

So single mama, do your thing. Wake up early, fix those lunches, get breakfast ready, wake your children and spend some time with them. Work hard during the day and set a schedule for the kids when they get home from school. Select the best childcare you can find and afford. Check up on the kids during the day. When you get home, get something quick, but balanced, together for dinner. Sit down to eat with your kids and talk to them about their day. Help with their homework. Get them ready for bed. Read to the little ones and let the older ones read some of their work to you. Lights go out early for them. Then take a couple of hours for yourself. Be disciplined and your children should follow your lead. Be a good single mama because you want to and you can. You are the heartbeat of so many communities. Do not ever forget that single mamas matter.

A final thought

Trash all the negative things anyone has ever told you about yourself. Write them down on a sheet of paper. Then tear it up in pieces and throw it away. Now, start thinking of the positive things that people tell you about yourself. Write those things down. Add to them some good things that you know about yourself, even if no one else has ever told you those things.

Take that sheet of paper and post it in a place that you see every day. Whenever you doubt yourself, take a look at those reminders of how wonderful you are.

With a mind clear of clutter and full of positive thoughts, you are in the best place to give your children what they so desperately need from their mama – strong arms and an open heart.